Anyone Can Pray

Anyone Can Pray

A GUIDE TO METHODS OF CHRISTIAN PRAYER

GRAEME J. DAVIDSON
with Mary Macdonald

illustrations by
William Hart McNichols

Paulist Press   *New York/Ramsey*

Library of Congress
Catalog Card Number: 82-62921

ISBN: 0-8091-2542-0

Published by Paulist Press
545 Island Road, Ramsey, N.J. 07446

Printed and bound in the
United States of America

CONTENTS

Contents

SECTION III

=====

SECTION IV

=====

SECTION V

=====

Contents

SECTION VI

Asian Prayer Techniques 115

SECTION VII

Praying With Others 131

SECTION VIII

Companions to Prayer 143

SECTION IX

Obstacles to Prayer 163

ACKNOWLEDGEMENTS

Excerpts from THE JERUSALEM BIBLE, copyright © 1966 by Darton, Longman & Todd, Ltd. and Doubleday & Company, Inc. Used by permission of the publisher.

Excerpts from THE REVISED STANDARD VERSION OF THE HOLY BIBLE, copyright © 1946, 1952, 1971, and 1973 by the Division of Christian Education of the National Council of the Churches of Christ in the U.S.A., and used by permission.

Reprinted by permission of ICS Publications from THE COLLECTED WORKS OF ST. TERESA OF AVILA, translated by Kieran Kavanaugh, O.C.D., and Otilio Rodriguez, O.C.D. (1976, 1980).

Reprinted by permission of ICS Publications from THE COLLECTED WORKS OF ST. JOHN OF THE CROSS, translated by Kieran Kavanaugh, O.C.D., and Otilio Rodriguez, O.C.D. (1979).

Reprinted by permission of Faber and Faber, Ltd. from THE ART OF PRAYER, compiled by Igumen Chariton of Valamo, translated by E. Kadloubovsky and E.M. Palmer (1978).

Reprinted by permission of Dawn Press/Simon and Schuster from HAPPINESS: THE TM PROGRAM, PSYCHIATRY, AND ENLIGHTMENT, written by Harold H. Bloomfield and Robert B. Kory (1976).

Reprinted by permission of Macmillan Publishing Co., Inc. from TONGUES OF MEN AND ANGELS, by William J. Samarin, copyright © 1972 by William J. Samarin.

Reprinted by permission of John Murray (Publishers) Ltd., from THE SPIRIT OF ZEN, by Alan Watts (1958) (U.S. edition published by Grove Press).

Reprinted by permission of the Institute of Jesuit Sources, from SADHANA: A WAY TO GOD, by Anthony de Mello (1979).

Reprinted by permission of Schocken Books, from LIGHT ON YOGA, by B.K.S. Iyengar, foreword by Yehudi Menuhin (1966).

The following Image books are reprinted by permission of Doubleday & Company, Inc.:

Excerpts from THE CLOUD OF UNKNOWING AND THE BOOK OF PRIVY COUNSELING, edited with an introduction by William Johnston (1973).

Excerpts from THE SPIRITUAL EXERCISES OF ST. IGNATIUS, translated by Anthony Mottola, introduction by Robert W. Gleason (1964).

Excerpts from THE STAIRWAY OF PERFECTION, by Walter Hilton, translated with an introduction by M.L. Del Mastro (1979).

Excerpts from THE WAY OF A PILGRIM AND THE PILGRIM CONTINUES HIS WAY, translated by Helen Bacovcin (1978).

Excerpts from THE PRACTICE OF THE PRESENCE OF GOD, by Brother Lawrence of the Resurrection, translated by John J. Delaney, foreword by Henri Nouwen (1977).

Excerpts from UPANISHADS: BREATH OF THE ETERNAL, selected and tr. by Swami Prabhavananda and Frederick Manchester, Mentor Books (1957), reprinted by permission of Vedanta Soc. of Southern California.

Excerpts from INTRODUCTION TO THE DEVOUT LIFE, St. Francis de Sales, translated and edited by John K. Ryan. Garden City, N.Y.: Image, 1972.

Excerpts from ZEN BUDDHISM: SELECTED WRITINGS OF D.T. SUZUKI, edited by William Barrett. Garden City, N.Y.: Doubleday Anchor, 1956.

To the Glory of God

PREFACE

Over recent years there has been an enormous upsurge of interest among Christians in spiritual matters. Retreat houses have waiting lists, spiritual directors have full appointment books, charismatic groups are flourishing, and religious periodicals have increased the numbers of articles they carry on prayer and other spiritual concerns. Many clergy with whom I have talked, in the United States and abroad, have mentioned their congregations' enormous hunger for expert spiritual guidance.

In the two parishes in which I worked in Southern California—one liberal, the other conservative—the most popular programs were classes on prayer and meditation. "I think," one of the participants explained, "that we Christians are realizing more and more that prayer is fundamental to living a life of faith. We can't love God properly unless we know how to communicate effectively with him."

Despite this keen interest in prayer, it can be difficult to find sound practical advice on how to pray. Most of us are shy about sharing our prayer experiences. Good spiritual teachers are hard to find. The numerous books and pamphlets on the subject tend either to be collections of other people's prayers, or to focus on the theory of prayer, or to be limited to a few specialized techniques. Many of the publications are aimed at only one denomination or interest group, while many writers use theological language which can be difficult to understand. Learning about the richness and diversity of Christian prayer methods can demand arduous study and amassing a small library—which few of us, however keen we are to learn about prayer, have time to do.

As a result many people do not extend their prayer horizons. My early prayer life was typical. I was brought up to repeat rote prayers, such as the Lord's Prayer, and to pour out to God what was on my mind. My prayers were entirely verbal. If I didn't have much to say I felt that I had failed. It wasn't until I was preparing for ordination that I gained an appreciation of contemplative silence, structured meditation, and the Jesus Prayer—other methods of praying which helped in developing a fuller relationship with God.

I have therefore seen a need for a basic "recipe book"—an easy-to-read, step-by-step guide to the wide range of prayer methods that are available. This book has been written to fulfill this need. It is a practical prayer guide to the major ways of prayer of the various Christian traditions—Protestant, Roman Catholic, and Eastern Orthodox—as well as Christian adaptations of some Asian techniques. I have included topics such as spiritual directors and teaching children to pray, as well as sections on the fundamental questions of why we pray and how to begin to pray so that the book will serve as a comprehensive text for both individuals and groups.

Anyone Can Pray is for anyone of high school age and onward who would like to develop his or her Christian prayer life. It is a useful companion to which we can refer for guidance and stimulus. As the book is practical and expansive in its scope, and each topic is short and self-contained, it will make an excellent text for classes and groups, as well as for the individual.

I have deliberately avoided suggesting that any technique is better than another. They are merely different. Each of us will prefer different styles of prayer, and will change these as our prayer life develops. Nevertheless, my own experience of teaching classes on prayer is that most Christians are reluctant to admit that they haven't really thought about something as basic as why they should pray, but are keen to learn about Zen. In spite of the greater allure of the exotic, I recommend that groups, in particular, using this book should start by considering the basic questions relating to prayer, and how each of us can pray using our own words. Therefore, although there is no progression from so-called "elementary" to "advanced" forms of prayer, and although each topic is self-contained, it would be advisable for a group to study the first three sections in sequence before looking at other topics. By beginning with a discussion on the fundamentals of prayer, the group members will be better prepared, and more enthusiastic and confident about trying out the methods and sharing their experiences. After all the best way to learn about prayer is to try it.

I feel certain that the procedures outlined in this book will help you to extend your prayer life and to grow in your love and devotion to God.

Graeme John Davidson
Santa Monica, California
December 1981

SECTION I

Why Pray?

ANYONE CAN PRAY

Anyone can pray. It is as simple as having a conversation with your best friend. You don't need a special kind of intellect, personality, or physical attributes. People of all ages and conditions can pray. I have listened to the simple prayers of a mongoloid child and the almost inarticulate utterances of a bedridden quadriplegic. Jesus selected ordinary people—fishermen, freedom fighters, and a tax collector—as his disciples, and taught them how to pray. If they could learn, we can do the same.

It isn't hard. All you need is the right attitude—humility and a genuine desire to communicate with God. That is all it takes. From the moment you really want to make contact with God you have already begun to pray.

You might think you have little to say to God, that you quite literally haven't a prayer. But you don't have to say much. There are many ways of praying. You can voice a simple cry, meditate on the Gospel message, reflect on creation, write a letter, or contemplate God's presence in silence. As in any dynamic relationship, you need to remain flexible in how you communicate.

God is the best friend you will ever have. His love for us is such that we can always rely on him to listen to our prayers. His appointment book is never so full that he can't fit us in. The psalmist knew this when he wrote, "The Lord is near to all who call upon him, to all who call upon him in truth" (Ps 145:18).

WHY PRAY?

The answer is simple. We pray to God because we love him and because he loves us. People in love enjoy being close to each other. If I told you how much I love my wife, and then added that I hadn't bothered to communicate with her for the last couple of years, you would doubt my sincerity. Yet I have met plenty of Christians who claim to love God but haven't been in touch for years.

You can't love God by proxy. He wants to hear from *you*. It is only by becoming fully involved that you will be able to enjoy an intimate relationship with him. You can share all your thoughts, feelings, and experiences—your joys, sorrows, problems, fears, hopes, and failures—in the full knowledge that God will understand and love you. When Jesus commanded us to love the Lord our God with all our heart, soul, and mind (Mt 22:37), he meant that we should commit ourselves wholeheartedly to God. God will continue to love you even if you treat him badly. You can always rely on his love.

Frequently we cast aside our Lord's first commandment in favor of the second, of loving our neighbor as ourselves (Mt 22:39). The needs of those around us appear so pressing and obvious that we give them priority. As society judges us by our good deeds and social actions rather than by the quality of our spiritual life, we find it easy to neglect prayer.

While it is essential that we care for others, our love and concern should involve more than an act of humanism. It needs to flow from our loving, close relationship with God. If not, we become like the overworked family man who is so occupied in his spare time with charitable projects that he allows his relationship with his loved ones to deteriorate. Far from inhibiting our outreach, our active love for others will be enhanced if we pray regularly. The Albert Schweitzers and Mother Teresas of this world have been fueled by prayer. They, along with countless Christians, stress that it has been through prayer that they have been able to accomplish so much. St. Augustine put this succinctly: "He that loveth little, prayeth little; he that loveth much, prayeth much."

Jesus' own prayer life is an excellent example to follow. He prayed frequently and taught us to pray—the Lord's Prayer. He also made the outstanding assertion: "If you have faith, every-thing you ask for in prayer you will receive" (Mt 21:22). To illus-trate what he meant, Jesus pointed to a mountain and claimed that by prayer it could be cast into the sea. Some of us have ac-cepted this saying at face value and believe that if we muster up enough faith, God will act on our behalf. While working as a jour-nalist I remember reporting on an airplane crash. "As we started to take off down the runway," one of the survivors recalled, "I knew we were in serious trouble. So for the first time since I was a kid, I prayed. I don't mind admitting it. I prayed like mad." As this man felt powerless he had turned to prayer as others might turn to positive thoughts, a rabbit's foot, or some other form of lucky charm. Some of us view prayer in a similar way. When technology fails, nations are on the brink of war, people we love have incurable illnesses, or we haven't done enough study for an exam, we look to God miraculously to bridge the gap, or move the mountain. We sometimes expect that our prayers will cause God to act like a supergenie, that he will provide an instant solu-tion. We forget that the reverse is true. Prayer is not a matter of manipulating God to respond to our will, but of opening our-selves to him, so that we become the instruments of *his* will. God uses us to answer our own prayers. With this view in mind, many Christians have opted for a metaphorical interpretation of Jesus' comment about the mountain being cast into the sea through prayer. The "mountain" Jesus refers to would be a figure of speech for some of the problems we face. That implies that if we trust God, he will lead us to an answer. He will point us in the right direction so that if we need to remove the mountain, the Holy Spirit will provide a way. These days that could mean using modern engineering techniques. However Jesus' illustration is to be understood, prayer can have an enormous impact on the world.

People throughout the ages have made remarkable claims for prayer—from the miraculous healing of incurable diseases and the conversion of hardened criminals to the making of right decisions or giving direction to an otherwise aimless life. One elderly woman whom I visited complained about feeling lonely and worthless. She was in constant pain from arthritis and had great difficulty in moving about her small apartment. When she told me how desperate she felt, I reminded her of the first commandment and suggested that she spend her time coming to know God through prayer and study. At first she was skeptical. She wanted to do something more practical. I had to assure her that if she came to God in prayer, she would experience the joy of his love, and this would give purpose to her life. As the weeks passed and she became occupied with her devotions, she started to radiate a sense of inner peace, joy, and love. Neighbors noticed the change. Instead of a tiresome and embittered old woman, she had become welcome company. Some even began to re-examine their own faith. Everyone benefited from her prayer life.

God doesn't always give us peace and inner strength when we pray, nor should we expect this. At one point the psalmist complains that he derives no comfort from his prayers:

> My soul refuses to be comforted.
> I think of God, and I moan;
> I meditate, and my spirit faints (Ps 77:2–3).

We, too, can lose heart when we don't seem to be receiving instant answers to our prayers. But don't give up; it sometimes takes time. God reveals his answer only when we are ready to receive it. He may even challenge and test us, as he did Job. Jesus and St. Paul urge us to have faith and be persistent in prayer. We need to persevere, not because God needs to be reminded of our problems, but so that we can remain continually open to his direction.

We often pray for peace in the world, and many of us must despair when yet another outbreak of hostilities occurs. But we should always have hope. If we persevere in our prayers, God will show us what part we can play to bring about a just peace. You might be led to raise questions to a political representative about your country's foreign policy, or contribute to refugee relief, or lend support for a negotiated settlement. You may feel powerless, but never underestimate what God can do through you.

Prayer enables us to put our worries and concerns into proper perspective. William James, the American psychologist, even prescribed prayer as "the sovereign cure for worry." When we approach God with our problems, we know that he will listen and understand. We can unburden ourselves to him and share what is on our mind. That in itself can be of great comfort. We also find that once we pour out our troubles to God, things start to fall into place as we concentrate on his boundless love.

Why should we bother to pray to God, when, as Jesus said, "Your Father knows what you need before you ask him" (Mt 6:8)? If God already knows what we need, surely it is presumptuous and redundant to pray to him? But although he knows what we are thinking, that doesn't mean we should neglect prayer. If we never pray, we shut ourselves off from a unique relationship and a chance to learn his will for us. As the Danish philosopher, Søren Kierkegaard, wrote: "Prayer does not change God, but changes the one who prays."

WHAT'S YOUR EXCUSE?

We can always make excuses for why we haven't prayed. Most of us would like to pray more than we do, but somehow we never get around to it. We are too tired, something else crops up, or else we are not in the right mood. Priests and pastors who hear private confessions say that failing to pray is the most frequent fault they hear. Recent surveys have shown that the clergy, who should be practiced in the art of prayer, seriously neglect their private devotions. Like the disciples who couldn't stay awake to pray with Jesus, our "spirit is willing, but the flesh is weak" (Mk 14:32f).

Our inertia can be overcome. It's a question of getting started. Often we feel so embarrassed about our lack of prayer that we are incapable of beginning. We feel so hypocritical and uncomfortable approaching God that we avoid the issue. As a result, a stand-off develops. There is only one way to break this impasse. We have to learn to accept that God is always glad to hear from us. Once you have broken the ice, you will find that you really are loved and accepted. You may even be a little more eager the next time. Like the father of the prodigal son that Jesus spoke of (Lk 15:11f), God will welcome you with open arms.

Even though we will be warmly received, many of us still can't believe that God will accept us. One graduate student who came to her priest in tears confessed that she had finally given in to her passions and slept with her boyfriend. She was very upset about the affair, and claimed that it was impossible for her to face God. She knew from the Bible that Jesus offered sinners hope and forgiveness, but somehow she believed that it wouldn't apply to her. She needed to be reassured that our Lord's love extended to her. Some critics accuse the Church of instilling an unhealthy sense of shame and guilt. They seem to ignore that the whole thrust of our faith is toward God's loving acceptance, no matter what we have done. Far from being burdened down with destructive emotions like guilt, we should be radiating God's love.

Our doubts can act as a major block to prayer. Questions about God's existence, his relationship with us, and the value of prayer often interfere. It is hard to pray to God if you believe he has gone into hibernation. Yet, our lack of faith need not be an insurmountable barrier. Jesus understood Thomas' skepticism about the resurrection—and Thomas was one of the disciples! Surely God will help us with our doubts if we let him know what we are thinking. Unless we ask for it, how can we be open to God's direction? Our doubts can be as much the subject of prayer as any other topic, so don't hesitate to confront God with your doubts. The father of the epileptic boy possessed of an evil spirit (Mk 9:14f) cried out to Jesus, "I do have faith. Help the little faith I have!" You should be as honest with God.

There will probably be stages in your life when you will be so riddled with doubts that you will barely be able to utter a word to God. Ernest Renan must have prayed the ultimate doubter's prayer, when he wrote:

> O Lord, if there is a Lord,
> Save my soul, if I have one.

At least he was still praying! He was being honest with God, and that's what you should be. Don't expect your doubts to disappear overnight. You need to persevere and follow Jesus' advice to "pray continually and never lose heart" (Lk 18:1).

At times we can become angry with God. We blame him for our problems. One girl who was born with a defective heart in my parish in England died prematurely at the age of ten. When I visited the mother, she turned on me in rage and told me in no uncertain terms what she thought of God for having taken her daughter. She certainly didn't seem in the mood to pray! But why shouldn't we confront God with our anger? We can become upset and frustrated with God, especially when our will clashes with his. At these times you should share your anger with God, not withdraw from him. This is the way to reconcile yourself with him.

Most of us are apprehensive about coming before God. He is beyond our comprehension, yet we have to put our trust in him and let him take control. We lay ourselves open to being challenged and transformed. We are exposed to his judgment, and this can be frightening. The closer we come to God, the more we become aware of the contrast between our shortcomings and his majesty. Because of this gulf between us and God, Archbishop Anthony Bloom of the Orthodox Church describes prayer as a dangerous adventure. He says that we put ourselves at risk whenever we approach God, and that we need courage to pray.

Of one thing you can be certain: the encounter will never leave you the same.

SECTION II

Beginning To Pray

FINDING THE TIME

The time to pray, we have often been told, is on rising and before going to bed. This advice is commonly given so that we can begin and end the day in God's presence. It is an excellent ideal, and if you are one of those who is wide awake at both ends of the day, you should try praying the first thing in the morning and the last thing at night. If you have sufficient discipline—and fortitude—you might even go so far as to break up your sleep in order to have a nocturnal prayer session. This was a custom of the early Church, and it has been recommended by some present day writers who claim that the practice leaves them feeling spiritually and physically refreshed.

But let's be honest. Many of us are half-asleep when we get out of bed or too exhausted after a long day at work. We need to find realistic times when we can be alert and give God our full attention.

Although you can pray at any time, you should have some fixed prayer periods scheduled throughout the day. Instead of praying at the crack of dawn, you could reorganize your routine and pray after you have showered and dressed, or even after breakfast. In the evening you might pray after your meal, or before you go out or settle down to watch television. You could also pray at lunch time, during a coffee break, or while commuting to and from work. Don't forget the shorter forms of prayer that can be used in any spare moment.

In his First Letter to the Thessalonians, Paul instructed them to "pray constantly" (1 Thes 5:17). That seems like a tall order. But

Paul wasn't expecting us to spend twenty-four hours a day on our knees. What he emphasized is that we should aim to make our whole life a prayer, that we should live our lives in God's presence.

When we love someone, we usually want to alter our lives to fit in with that person who becomes the focus of our attention. To follow Paul's instructions, you will need to make God the center of your being. You should be constantly aware that you are in God's presence, so that everything you do becomes a prayer. This idea is embodied in the motto of the Benedictine order, "Ora et labora"—pray and work. This could become your ideal, but watch out that you don't substitute work for prayer. There are plenty of Christian activists who are so busy doing the Lord's work that they have little time to spend with God. Try to avoid this trap!

CHOOSING A PLACE

You can pray anywhere. You don't have to be surrounded by stained glass windows and pews or be looking at one of the seven wonders of the world. Jesus certainly didn't confine his praying to the temple or synagogues. He prayed in a garden, on a mountain top, in the desert, by a lake, before meals, in a lonely place, at the Last Supper, and on the cross.

Throughout history, people have selected some extraordinarily diverse places in which to pray. Simon the Stylite (390–459) spent thirty-six years on a sixty-foot pillar in Syria so that he could be free from worldly temptations to concentrate on God. Thalelaeus of Cilicia (c. 450) endured ten years cramped up in a wooden cage in prayers of penitence. Similarly, in the sixth century, Bishop Kentigern of Scotland often prayed all one hundred and fifty psalms in one session, frequently standing in an ice cold stream. The solitude of the desert has attracted many. In the third century, the Desert Fathers of Egypt lived as hermits in the wilderness. More recently the French spiritual writer, Charles de Foucauld, became a hermit in the Algerian Sahara, while the famous rocket pioneer, Werner von Braun, often interrupted his work to take long rides into the desert to pray. A humble Carmelite monk, Brother Lawrence (1611–1691), worked twenty years in the monastery kitchen before it dawned on him that God was always present and he could pray just as well among the pots and pans. He expressed this in one of his letters:

> It is not necessary to be always in church to be with God;
> we can make a private chapel of our heart where we can
> retire from time to time to commune with him, peace-

fully, humbly, lovingly; everyone is capable of these intimate conversations with God, some more, others less
(*The Practice of the Presence of God*, 4th letter).

Although we can pray anywhere, it helps if we have special
places for prayer. Jesus told us:

> When you pray, go to your private room and, when you
> have shut your door, pray to your Father who is in that
> secret place, and your Father who sees all that is done in
> secret will reward you (Mt 6:6).

He gives us this advice because he didn't want us to emulate the
Pharisees, who were more interested in making a public display
of their piety than in communicating with God.

Prayer Corner

As a youngster, I was taught, like many of us, to pray kneeling at my bedside before going to sleep. When I went to boarding school and had to sleep in a large dormitory, I tried to continue this practice. I was subjected to a barrage of football boots, books, and anything else that was at hand, and roughly told by my fellow boarders that I was showing off and they were not in the least impressed. I considered myself a martyr; in fact, I was more of a Pharisee.

Your "secret place" could be a corner of your home, such as a spare room, bedroom, study, or other quiet place which should provide sufficient uninterrupted privacy. You will need to include your Bible, other devotional reading, and any helpful aids to meditation, such as pictures or religious articles in your prayer corner. It could be worthwhile to have several alternative sites. One could be out of doors: in a park, on a hillside, at the beach or by a stream. Another location could be a favorite chapel; this need not necessarily be your own local church. You could choose any empty room at the office or the public library; you might even consider praying while commuting to and from work. Whichever places you select should help you come closer to God.

POSITIONS

You can pray in practically any position. Some people prefer to kneel, others to lie prostrate, while a few Christian yogis will even pray standing on their heads! It is just a question of finding the positions that best suit your needs. If you are at a church service, unless you want to stand out from the other worshipers, then the choices are normally limited to sitting, kneeling, or standing. In the Eastern Orthodox Church, there are also occasions when you could choose to lie prostrate on the floor. I have heard many heated arguments about the merits of each position—as though any one of them would be better at attracting God's attention!

Yet the posture can reflect our attitude to God. In the third century the Desert Fathers prayed standing with uplifted hands while facing the east. The uplifted hands symbolized the reception of the Holy Spirit, a practice which many charismatics have revived. The Celtic monks of the sixth century spent long hours standing in prayer with outstretched arms in what is known as the "crossfigell" position, to represent the crucified Christ, while in 813 the Synod of Tours demanded that public prayers be said while kneeling, "so that in this way we may crave God's mercy and have forgiveness of sins." In contrast many Protestant churches have no facilities for kneeling, since they believe that this overemphasizes our sinful nature rather than the joys of being saved. In most Orthodox churches, the few seats are usually taken by the infirm; everyone else stands, kneels, or lies. Seats, pews, and kneelers are comparatively recent innovations for most Christian churches.

Uplifted Hands

Many of us have been brought up to show respect for our Lord by either bowing our heads, kneeling, genuflecting, or bowing from the waist before or during prayer. In these ways we have learned to demonstrate that God is our Lord and King and that we are his dependent, humble servants. Whatever outward display you adopt, remember: it is your inner attitude that counts.

No matter what your theological outlook, you will need to be realistic about the physical positions you use for personal prayer. You could make the mistake of being too comfortable. Trying to pray while lying in the sun on a warm day might contribute to your tan, but could prove fatal to your concentration. Snuggling up in a cozy chair before a blazing fire could be equally detrimental.

Crossfigell Position

We can also go to the other extreme of deliberately making ourselves uncomfortable. In the thirteenth century Christina the As-
tonishing (the title is quite apt!) often prayed while balancing on a
hurdle or else curled up like a hedgehog on the ground. St. Patrick of Ireland is said to have risen during the night to pray a hundred psalms together with two hundred genuflections. Many
during the Middle Ages prayed while whipping themselves (flagellation) or undergoing some other kind of self-imposed ordeal.
Even today there are some who subject themselves to harsh practices in the belief that this will help them with their prayers.

But despite Jesus' suffering and his injunction that we must take
up our cross daily to follow him, we don't have to become mas-
ochists in order to pray. We need to find the middle ground and
adopt positions that best suit our physical needs, the length of

time we will spend in prayer, the type of prayer, and, of course, where we are.

For short periods of prayer virtually any position is possible. For longer sessions of prayer, especially for reflection, you will need to find a posture that can be maintained. For most of us this will mean sitting. Ideally this is best done on a padded chair with your back straight, but not rigid, feet resting on the floor, and your hands held loosely in your lap. You should aim to sit quite still in a relaxed manner.

If you prefer to kneel, then it might help to obtain a prayer stool or a prayer bench (*prie-dieu*), but make certain that what you choose is the right height for your body. You might consider using a cushion to kneel or sit upon while praying. A special type of cushion, or *zafu,* is often used by those who practice Zen. You

Prayer Bench

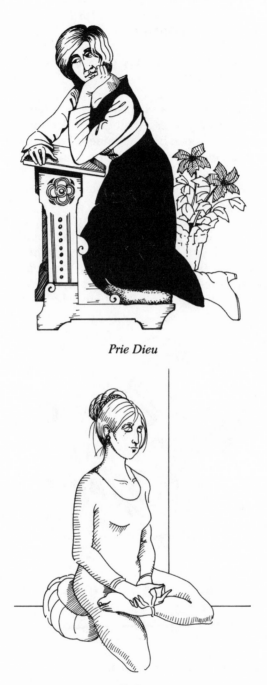

Prie Dieu

Zafu

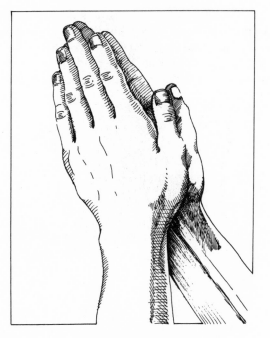

"Praying Hands"

could vary your routine by praying while walking in a garden or park.

You can bring your hands together in the traditional devotional pose made famous in the "Praying Hands" (actually entitled "Hands of an Apostle") drawing by Albrecht Dürer, or else raise your hands heavenward; but before long you will be reminded that the forces of gravity can make these positions tiring for lengthy prayer.

When we were first taught to pray, we were probably encouraged to close our eyes to shut out any visual distractions. The trouble with this was that the effort of keeping the eyes closed sometimes made us more curious about what was going on around us than before, especially during group prayer. So we would occasionally peek to see what others were doing, and whether they were peeking at us. Far from helping us to concentrate on God, shutting the eyes became a distraction. It certainly isn't necessary to close your eyes, but it is important that your attention be on God, not your surroundings. If shutting the eyes helps, then continue to do this. You could also try looking downward or gazing at a point in the distance. You will then be vaguely aware of what is going on around you, while your thoughts are raised to God.

MAKING CONTACT

How should we begin to pray? In much the same way we would begin a conversation with anyone we love. We start by giving God our attention and tuning in to him. When Jesus taught the disciples to pray, he began: "Our Father. . . ." He focused on God, making him the object of the prayer. Unless our attention is on God our prayer times will become pro forma affairs, empty formalities in which we go through the motions. If your prayers are to rise above the ceiling, or to be more than a monologue with yourself, then you must begin by centering on God, so that he may play a part in the communication.

It is not always easy to concentrate on God. The disciples went to sleep when Jesus asked them to pray in the Garden of Gethsemane, and most of us find that our minds will wander when we begin to pray. "I always start my prayers with the best of intentions," a friend of mine once told me, "but I can't help thinking of my wife and family, or the latest problems at work. God seems to get lost in the crowd." This man, like many of us, was plunging into prayer without taking a little time to prepare himself. Like an athlete who goes through a warm-up routine before a race, we too need to go through a warm-up procedure before launching directly into extended periods of prayer.

The psalmist gives the key to approaching our Lord when he urges us to "be still and know that I am God" (Ps 46:10). We need to relax and unwind, so that we can cast aside our daily preoccupations and center on God. So before launching directly into any extended periods of prayer, you might try the following warm-up, while sitting or lying in a comfortable position.

29

Begin by breathing slowly and deeply from the abdomen. Once you have established a rhythmic pattern of deep breathing, concentrate on relaxing the various parts of your body. Start with your feet, then move up to your calves, thighs, buttocks, stomach, arms, elbows, and hands, then along your spine and ribs to your neck, chin, face, tongue, forehead, and eyelids. Let go of all tension in your muscles until your body feels limp and heavy, as if it were detached. In recent years, yoga exercises have become popular as a warm-up procedure. Some of these methods could be considered as an alternative way of preparing the body for prayer. If you do have trouble relaxing, you might also try a warm bath before you pray.

To eliminate distractions and daily concerns that could cloud your openness to God, imagine yourself entering a tunnel which grows progressively darker and quieter, until at last you are alone in total darkness, alert and receptive, with no intrusions, sounds, or visual stimuli competing for your attention. Once you reach this stage, you are ready to give your undivided attention to God.

To fill yourself with an awareness of God's presence, picture the dark void filled with the warm light of God, surrounding you and shining through your entire body so that you feel his presence around and within you. If you find this image of the light too impersonal, try imagining that Jesus is somewhere there in the dark radiating a warmth and love that gradually engulfs you.

Another method for focusing on God is to concentrate on the various aspects of the Holy Trinity. Perhaps you could think about him as Creator, or else dwell on the love he has shown to us through his Son or on the continuing work of the Holy Spirit in our lives. Try not to restrict God to only one aspect of his personality. It might be easier to consider him in terms of the historical Jesus or the present day workings of the Holy Spirit; but to narrow God down to one short period of history is to take a lopsided view of the Holy Trinity. Of course, we can't expect to comprehend all of the divine. St. Paul tells us that at best all we can see is "a dim reflection in a mirror" (1 Cor 13:12), but we can aim for a balanced view of God.

After practice, you will find that you are able to center on God without extensive preparation. Once your attention is on God, and you feel that you are in his presence, ask the Holy Spirit to guide and direct you during your prayer time; then be silent and allow God to speak first.

In the same way that we would ask a friend to pray for us, Christians of some traditions will call upon a favorite saint for prayers to God on their behalf. The saint is not intended to be viewed as a minor deity, but functions as an aid to intercession.

Although Jesus told us to use his name when we make our prayer requests (Jn 14:13), we don't have to punctuate every line with his name. It is not as though there were many gods in a heavenly waiting room expecting their individual titles to be called at regular intervals before they will respond. There is only one God, and as soon as you focus on him, you have begun to pray.

Some of us prefer to use the old-fashioned "thee's" and "thou's" when we pray. I remember one pastor who was reprimanded by his congregation for using modern English at public worship. They told him it was irreverent to pray to God as if he were talking with his next door neighbor. The cleric responded by delivering the whole of his next Sunday's service, including the sermon, in perfect Elizabethan English! He had made his point. God doesn't have to be addressed in one fixed form of language. Originally the "thou" form was used in addressing family members and close friends. To modern ears it connotes a more remote, formal tone. If using sixteenth century English is comfortable and helps you to be more reverent, continue to use it. But don't let these older stylized forms of speech distance you from God. The language you use should be natural, not forced.

Although we can be intimate with God, prayer is not a conversation among equals. When Jesus referred to God as "Our Father," he highlighted the relationship we have with him: that of child to parent. God is our Creator who provides and cares for us. That means that we, his children, should approach him with love and respect. Jesus tells us:

> Unless you change and become like little children you
> will never enter the kingdom of heaven (Mt 18:3).

In our competitive free enterprise society, we have learned that worldly success usually comes from being self-reliant, confident, and demanding. This makes it difficult for many of us to adopt an attitude of humility. Yet, the only way to come before the throne of God is in openness, truthfulness, and humility. The anonymous writer of the Letter to the Hebrews stresses that we all stand naked before our Lord and Maker:

> No created thing can hide from him; everything is un-
> covered and open to the eyes of the one to whom we
> must give account of ourselves (Heb 4:13).

WHAT TO SAY

When the disciples asked Jesus to teach them to pray, he came up with a balanced approach which was God-centered, self-centered, and other-centered. We repeat the Lord's Prayer so often that we almost forget what the words mean. It is worth having a look at the prayer again:

Our Father, who art in heaven, hallowed be thy name.　Greeting and praise.

Thy kingdom come,　Hoping for God's rule.

Thy will be done,　Considering God's will for us,

on earth as it is in heaven.　and what we can do for him.

Give us this day our daily bread.　Asking for our needs.

And forgive us our trespasses, as we forgive those who trespass against us.　Confessing our sins and forgiving others.

And lead us not into temptation,　Requesting help to avoid sin.

But deliver us from evil.　Appealing for help to overcome
(cf. Mt 6:9–13)　evil.

We don't always have to repeat the words used by Jesus, and leave it at that. Why not try using his famous prayer as a model, a guide for the content of your own prayers? Although you should begin as Jesus did by focusing on God, adoring and praising him for all the great things he can do—remember God the Father, God the Son, and God the Holy Spirit—there is no special reason to follow the same order.

You will need to include prayers asking that God's will be done in the world. You could ask for the Holy Spirit's guidance in all your undertakings—work, recreation, family, or church. You might also pray for the unconverted and those floundering in the faith. Then be ready to listen to what God wants you to do to help bring about his rule. After all, there is little point in asking that his will be done if you are not prepared to play an active part. Don't leave all of God's work to a few hard workers.

When Jesus mentioned our daily bread he was referring to our everyday necessities—not luxuries! It is amazing how many people expect God to act like a Santa Claus. When I was a child, I prayed that God would give me a little car with an engine, lights, and a horn so that I could act grown-up and be the envy of all my friends. Since then I have heard people pray for sports cars, yachts, and mansions, as well as to win lotteries, football pools, the Super Bowl, and the Kentucky Derby. Of course we can all rationalize why we need these things, but don't be surprised if God says "No." In the First Letter of John, we are reminded that God hears us "if we ask him for anything, and it is in accordance with his will" (1 Jn 5:14). That would rule out prayers that are no more than self-indulgent fantasies.

As well as praying for employment, health, shelter, safety, and companionship, you should also include spiritual needs such as an increase in faith, greater capacity to love, and the ability to be a better witness for Christ. We are often so busy thinking in terms of our physical necessities that we can forget that our daily bread can include spiritual nourishment.

Jesus did not teach us to pray for "my daily bread" but "our daily bread." Our prayers should reflect our concern for the wider community—not just a few select friends. You can include prayers of intercession for the homeless, the unhappily married, unbelievers, the lonely, victims of war and violence, the sick and handicapped, the hungry, and justice for the oppressed. This will mean that if you are to pray effectively, you will have to become well informed about the real needs of the people in the world. As it is almost impossible to keep up to date with the whole spectrum of current world events, it is a good idea to concentrate on several issues and make these your special prayer concerns.

Your confessions of how you have hurt God and other people should include what you have done as well as what you have failed to do. Traditionally we have been encouraged to think in terms of the seven deadly sins—anger, envy, avarice, pride, lust, sloth, and gluttony—but don't restrict yourself to this list. Think about whatever has separated you from God, and humbly ask for forgiveness.

As a community we can also offend God—in the ways we treat the elderly, certain racial and ethnic groups, other nations, social misfits, and the environment. Don't forget to include these corporate or community sins as well. Although confession will take up part of your prayer time, it is not advisable to linger over your sins. Accept that they are past and forgiven.

You will also need to forgive others. This can be hard, as some people have the knack of getting under our skin. When I was employed as a prison psychologist in New Zealand, I counseled a man who was sentenced for child molesting. He prayed for God's mercy, then wrote to the family of the girl he had sexually assaulted asking to be forgiven, and offering half his savings for her education. Although the parents were leaders of their local church, they couldn't find it in their hearts to forgive. They refused to have anything more to do with the prisoner and demanded retribution. His sentence, they complained, was too light and he should have been forced to undergo a sex operation. To dramatize the importance of forgiving others, Jesus told a similar story of an unforgiving debtor (Mt 18:23f), and talked about forgiving seventy times seven and turning the other cheek.

Most of us have some insight into weaknesses and are aware of what leads us away from God. When you examine your sins, take note of how you were led astray and ask for God's help in avoiding these situations. If gluttony is your problem, tell God about your addiction to food or drink, and ask for strength and guidance in overcoming this temptation. Be open to God's direction. The first move might be to get medical advice or join a support group. It is worth bearing in mind what St. Paul tells us—that God will sometimes put temptation in our way to test our faith. But he assures us that through God's grace we will be strengthened and able to meet the challenge.

> You can trust God not to let you be tried beyond your strength, and with any trial he will give you a way out of it and the strength to bear it (1 Cor 10:13).

People have different ideas about the existence of an evil one or a devil. But whatever your stand on this issue, we can agree that there is evil in the world. There are tragic accidents, illness, and natural disasters, as well as the horrific inhumanity that we inflict on each other. Christians have even been guilty of cruelty in the name of Christ. Often we shut our eyes to these evils in the hope that they will go away. We want to escape to an imaginary Garden of Eden and pretend that the fall never happened. Pray for victims of accidents and violence, the sick, the bereaved, and the oppressed and their oppressors.

As our own attitudes can contribute to evil, you will need to take a good honest look at yourself. Do you drive recklessly, endangering other people? Do you get a vicarious thrill out of watching violent television programs? You need to be open to the possibility of being an instrument for evil. On a world scale, your contribution might look very small, but cumulatively it all adds up.

Whatever you pray for, you will need to be specific. If we pray for everything in general, we pray for nothing in particular. On the other hand, if we are too detailed, we border on the ridiculous, asking God to decide on trivial matters.

Another popular prayer model is referred to by the acronym ACTS. This stands for adoration, confession, thanksgiving, and supplication (prayers of request). All four elements of ACTS, with the possible exception of thanksgiving, have already been mentioned in connection with the Lord's Prayer. Thanksgiving can be implied in our praise and adoration. But it is also a good idea to give special thanks to God. Most of the Jewish prayers of Jesus' time were those of praise and thanksgiving. They didn't take God for granted—and neither should you.

If you cannot think of anything to say to God, don't let this worry you. "For when we cannot choose words in order to pray properly," St. Paul assures us, "the Spirit himself expresses our plea in a way that could never be put into words, and God who knows everything in our hearts knows perfectly well what he means . . ." (Rom 8:26–27). Just being with God could be your prayer.

WHICH METHOD?

There are many prayer methods. It's a question of finding the most appropriate style for you. Some methods are designed for fleeting moments, some for an entire weekend, others for meditating on the Gospel, or for wordless contemplation. Prayer can include letter writing, dancing, singing, glossolalia (speaking in tongues), the rosary, group meditation, mantras, and even watching television. Much of the rest of this book is devoted to explaining these methods.

You may be using some of these techniques already and feel hesitant about trying something different, especially if it is from outside your prayer tradition. Some of us become uneasy at the mention of the rosary, praying in tongues, Zen meditation, or the constant repetition of the Jesus Prayer. But we shouldn't become so defensive about our own particular brand of prayer that we block off other avenues to God.

One young man told me that all he had to do to pray was sit down and start talking to God. I asked him, "Do you communicate with your wife by talk alone? Don't you sometimes write letters, telephone, touch her, go dancing, or just be silent together?" He realized what I was getting at. There is more than one way of approaching God and we need to be flexible.

This doesn't mean that we should swing to the other extreme and rush into all the methods at once. They are only a means to an end, a way of coming into contact with God. Contact should be your priority. You are not trying to rack up points on a heavenly scoreboard by impressing God with your spiritual expertise.

Another hazard is that we can theorize about prayer and discuss the advantages and disadvantages of each method, but never get around to actually praying. Avoid becoming an armchair critic. Learn about prayer firsthand.

Treat this book as you would a cookbook of recipes. After flicking through the pages, you could select one or two methods that are new to you and work with them for a while before moving on to another technique. Be patient. These procedures can also be tailored to your individual circumstances. Whatever method you adopt, I hope that your prayer life will be enriched.

SECTION III

Prayer in Your Own Words

CRIES TO GOD

God is willing to listen to anyone who calls out to him. The psalmist reminds us: "The Lord is near to all who call upon him, to all who call upon him in truth" (Ps 145:18). You don't necessarily have to stick to a scheduled prayer time or have a prepared agenda. Nor do you have to use your best formal prose. God is not a grammar teacher ready to give you a low grade for incomplete sentences or not reaching a thousand words. He listens just as much to the heartfelt cry or a hastily murmured phrase as he does to the beautifully crafted prayers of the poet or the carefully formulated prayers of a religious organization.

We strive so often to imitate the prayers of others that we can turn prayer into an intellectual exercise. We tend to ignore our feelings, what the psalmist calls the "cries of the heart." Yet there are plenty of occasions when words escape us, when we are at a loss to know what to say. Often we feel so emotionally moved that all we can do is make a simple exclamation like "Isn't that fantastic?" or "How awful!" A depth of feeling and meaning is conveyed by the way they are spoken, so why not use them as prayers to God?

After hearing that her daughter had been seriously injured in a car accident, all that one woman could say as she rushed to be by her daughter's side was, "Oh God! My God! Be with her!" She repeated the words, out loud and to herself, over and over. Everything she felt was in that prayer—her love for her daughter, her anxiety and concern, as well as her simple request to God. Of course, you don't have to wait for a crisis. A cry can be used just as effectively when you feel happy, in love, or overwhelmed by the magnificence of nature. When I visited the Grand Canyon, my initial response was, "What a creation! Thanks, God!" Other people might say "Hallelujah!" or "Praise the Lord!" These joyous cries all suggest the same thing—that God is being praised for his magnificent creation.

If you are frightened, angry, unhappy about a mistake, or suffering from the pangs of guilt, why not turn these negative feelings into short prayers? A plain "I've sinned!" or "I've messed that up, Lord!" or "Oh God!" can convey all that you feel. You have spontaneously offered your feelings to God. They are your prayers, pure and simple.

Don't be put off using these spontaneous cries to God because so many people use the names of God and Jesus when they curse and swear. Even if you do say "Jesus" or "Oh God," it doesn't mean that you are automatically uttering a profanity. God forbid! It all depends on your intentions. If you are offering a genuine sentiment to God, you are using the words as they were intended. If you are worried that you will be misunderstood by those who might overhear you, then a silent cry is just as effective. The aim of any prayer is to communicate with God, not to impress the neighbors with our piety.

Many devoted Christians, including mystics, make use of this prayer technique. In just a few words, they focus all their feelings, emotions, and intellect on God. One of the early Desert Fathers, St. John Cassian, often prayed by saying, "O Lord, help me!" while the twentieth century mystic, Padre Pio, repeated "Jesus! Mary!" as he lay on his deathbed. Some devout people will exclaim, "God be praised!" or "Amen!" or "Maranatha!" (Come, Lord Jesus!). These words are not trite expressions, but are packed with meaning and associations. One word on the lips of a believer can be very profound. A short, spontaneous utterance can be the most effective of prayers, for if one cry from the heart can say it all, why be long-winded?

ONE-LINERS

If you have a few moments to spare, why not compose a simple prayer? It need only be a one line sentence—or even a question to God. It is like sending a telegram: you get straight to the point. You don't have to spend time producing a polished literary effort. Just say what you want to say and leave it at that.

At a wedding breakfast I was asked to say the grace. I simply said, "Thank you, Lord, for this happy occasion and for the food we are about to eat. Amen." Everyone burst out laughing. They felt short-changed. My brief thanksgiving wasn't enough. They expected that as a clergyman I should have been able to produce a few extra flourishes. What they didn't seem to realize was that what matters is not the number of words we offer to God but the sincerity of those words. Martin Luther, the Protestant reformer, even contended that the shorter prayers are the best. "The fewer the words," he said, "the better the prayer."

You will need to think about what you are praying. Unlike a cry to God, which is usually a spontaneous emotional outpouring, a one-liner requires thought. It is going to be more of a planned response than a gut reaction. You can turn practically anything into a short prayer. It can be the boss at work, a crying baby, a nostalgic memory, a dollar bill, the police officer who just passed you in a patrol car, or a trip to the supermarket.

Once when I was in the supermarket, I had my eye on a package of fancy cookies. I really didn't need them, but they did look enticing. I thought of an appropriate prayer, and before I had finished uttering, "Thank you, God, for our daily bread" (because it

was very hard to formulate a prayer about cookies), I had my answer. My daily bread was already in the shopping basket. So I
thought of others who were not so fortunate, and put the money
aside for hunger relief. This story raises another point about one-
liners. In thinking about what to say, you are listening to God as
well. It is worth pausing a few moments after your prayer. You
never know what God might want to say.

Your prayer-sentences don't always have to be statements. We often ask questions throughout the day, so why not ask questions of
God? While in a book shop, perhaps you could ask, "What reading material would be best for me, Lord?" Once you have raised
this question, it is surprising how your criteria for books and mag-
azines can change. You can hardly be serious about your question
if you choose a steady diet of cheap thrillers and pornography.

If you are worried about your children's behavior, why not a sentence, "Show me, heavenly Father, how to set them a loving example." If you see an ambulance speeding by, instead of being
annoyed at having to pull over, why not say a prayer for the victim or give a short thanks for the paramedics?

When you are going through a dry spell during your scheduled
prayer time, one-liners are an ideal way of keeping your prayer
life alive. Any of your thoughts can be turned into an instant
prayer, even your anti-social fantasies. One man, thinking nega-
tively about his boss, decided to offer a short prayer about it. He
prayed, "I dislike this man intensely. What should I do about this,
Lord?" Within a few seconds he had the answer. He had a mental
image of Jesus dying on the cross for all people, including his persecutors. He realized that Jesus' loving sacrifice extended to his
boss as well as him.

By using short prayers, sometimes called arrow or ejaculatory
prayers, you can keep in touch with God throughout the day.
This makes it possible, even if you are very busy, to begin to approach Paul's ideal of constant prayer.

SAYING MORE

There will be plenty of times when you will need to pray more than a sentence or two—especially if there is something on your mind. You might want to say a lot about your marriage, the crime rate, unemployment, or the local church, or to give thanks to God for his blessings. Moreover, few of us are so saintly that we could reduce our confessions to a one-liner.

Having much to say is one thing, but being able to say it is quite another. Many of us dry up when we approach God in prayer. After the first couple of sentences, we get stuck. We don't know what to say next. We grind to a halt, or go off on a tangent, and never get around to saying what is on the tip of our tongues. It is similar to what used to happen when I first placed international telephone calls home to New Zealand. After the initial excited greeting, neither party knew quite what to say next. Before the call, my mind was crammed with things to say, but once I made contact, they all seemed to evaporate. Instead we ended up in expensive conversations about the weather. It didn't take long to realize that in the future I would need to have a few notes at hand if I wanted to avoid unnecessary meteorological discussions.

The same technique can be used when we are at a loss for words while communicating with God. Unless you have an excellent memory, why not think ahead and jot down a few key points on a note pad? This will be a useful reminder of the topics you want to cover. Once you have a few notes, you can develop your thoughts into lengthier prayer conversations.

The best way to do this is by association. Take the material that you have noted, recall particular examples, and include them in your prayers. Don't be vague; be specific. If you made a note to give thanks for your job, then you could associate this with your income, talents, health, and the companionship of your colleagues. You could also think in terms of how your work contributes to the welfare of the community, and give thanks to God. You could then generalize to others. Perhaps you could pray for workers in your neighborhood, unions and management associations, honesty at work, industrial safety, the unemployed, and those unhappy in their work. In this way, your prayers can be broadened to others, even if you begin with yourself. Once you have outlined the situation to God, you can then ask for his guidance. Be ready to be led by the Holy Spirit. This can take the form of inventing a new safety procedure, or befriending that unhappy co-worker.

Most topics can be handled in the same manner. If you have noted a tendency to stuff yourself with food, begin your prayer by mentioning when and what you overeat, the likely consequences to your health, how this could affect your responsibilities, and why you think you give in to this temptation. Then ask for God's help and guidance. When you broaden your associations, you could pray about obesity, malnutrition, those who work to solve these problems, and the two-thirds of the world that is starving, and give thanks for the wonderful selection and availability of good food for you. This will put your temptation into a wider perspective so that you can be more open to the direction of the Holy Spirit.

It is worth keeping your notes. They can serve as a prayer outline for other occasions. Check that your prayers are balanced; remember to include adoration, confession, thanksgiving, and supplication (see *What To Say*). Other material can also act as a stimulus to prompt you to pray—the Bible, religious art, music, nature, etc. (see *Media Prayer, The Scrapbook, Learning To Meditate, Reflecting on Nature,* and *Props and Customs*). You could think about exchanging your outlines with fellow Christians. Don't be shy about sharing your prayers. We can learn from each other.

MEDIA PRAYER

You can turn your television viewing into a time of prayer. A shocking news story, a dramatic presentation—even the commercials—can be incorporated into your prayers. You can be transformed from a passive viewer to an active prayerful participant. The procedure is quite simple. First, watch a program and absorb what is going on. Effective prayer requires that you be well informed. Then pray for all those involved. Next, think of similar situations, and include them in your prayers. Finally, ask God for guidance.

Suppose an act of terrorism is featured on the news. As the motives of the victims, the authorities, and the terrorists are revealed, you can mention them in your prayers. Don't let the plight of the victims close your mind to the problems of the attackers. God cares about everyone. You would then extend your prayers to those involved in similar incidents elsewhere and ask God for a just and peaceful settlement.

A nature documentary can be treated in the same way. Here, you might pray for the forms of life that are portrayed and the specialists concerned with their preservation and research. You could then praise and thank God for the wonder of his creation and ask to be guided in using these natural resources wisely.

Insofar as dramatic presentations mirror contemporary life and values, we can also turn to them as a source of prayer. If you are disgusted by the routine fare of dramatized violence, sex, exploitation, and material goals, pray about this and switch to another channel. An aspirin advertisement might stimulate prayers for

49

human suffering and relief, but you could also use the time-out for the sponsor's message as a mini-meditation period.

You can use the same techniques while listening to the radio or reading a newspaper. Many Christians have told me that they make their intercessions while following the news on their car radio. The big advantage of the print medium is that you can refer back to the material and share it with others. You can always use what you have learned for later prayers. Perhaps you might include clippings and articles in a prayer scrapbook.

THE SCRAPBOOK

Most of us collect photos, clippings, cards, poems, and anything else that has made a strong impression on us. You could just as easily create an album which would prompt you to pray. This would be your own distinctive prayerbook. Start with an empty book and add whatever will lead you to think about God.

Don't feel that you have to stick to postcard reproductions of Leonardo da Vinci's Last Supper. My personal book includes photographs of the family, godchildren, friends, my home and garden, and places and people throughout the world. It also contains postcards of Christian art and architecture, baptism, confirmation and ordination certificates, Christmas and birthday cards, letters, prayers and quotations, religious jokes and cartoons, an olive leaf from the Garden of Gethsemane, and a palm cross made for me by a small boy on an oasis in the Sahara Desert. Other Christians have included pictures of their pets, a favorite member of the clergy, or a patron saint, the names of their graduating class, and their own religious art work. Favorite recordings and inspirational tapes have been used to the same end.

You can use your scrapbook in much the same way as prayer notes or media material. Let your mementos act as a stimulus to prayer. Pick a subject and make your associations. A baptismal certificate could promote meditation and prayer about being born anew in Jesus Christ, while a photograph of old friends could elicit prayers for their present well-being. On the other hand, a palm cross or a religious art work could be the basis for a sustained in-depth meditation.

The scrapbook format is not the only way to display your material. One family I know uses their refrigerator door in place of an album. You might try this, or else share some of your objects on a home bulletin board. In these cases the scrapbook can become a family affair.

IMAGINING HIS PRESENCE

How often have you felt that God was remote from you when you prayed? You know he is listening, but because he isn't tangible, he doesn't seem real. As children we might have pictured God as a wise grandfatherly figure sitting on a throne in the sky. Now that we recognize that he is everywhere, we have modified this simple image. We steer clear of forcing God into a human mold. But in our desire to be more theologically sophisticated, aren't we in danger of throwing out the wheat with the chaff? God came to us in human form through his Son, so why not imagine that we are talking to Jesus when we pray?

You could picture him as a parent, counselor, companion, colleague, or close friend—someone who is caring and is prepared to listen sympathetically. St. Teresa of Avila (1515–1582), who changed the course of sixteenth century spiritual life, suggested that we envisage God as a head or a member of the family, and that we vary our imagery:

> . . . speak with Him as with a father, or a brother, or a lord, or as with a spouse; sometimes in one way, at other times in another . . . (*The Way of Perfection,* 28:3).

However you picture Jesus, don't get lost in a mass of visual detail. You could become so engrossed in the color of his beard, his height, and whether he was wearing first century or modern clothes that your prayers become secondary. To eliminate this distraction, it is probably just as well to avoid a face-to-face encounter. You could depict Jesus as the voice at the other end of the telephone, as a therapist who sits just out of sight, or as a com-

panion at your side. One young Christian told me that she imag-
ines Jesus as a jogging partner. Another has mentioned that
whenever he has difficulty praying, he visualizes Jesus as a shad-
owy figure coming toward him and greeting him warmly. They
then walk together along the beach or in a park.

On a holiday in Scotland, I joined a family for their Christmas
dinner. There were fifteen people and sixteen chairs. When I
asked if someone was missing, they explained that the empty
chair symbolized the unseen guest, who was Christ.

We should also recognize that since God is everywhere he is
within us. To quote St. Teresa again, "All one need do is go into
solitude and look at Him within oneself, and not turn away from
so good a Guest but with great humility speak to Him as to a father" (*The Way of Perfection,* 28:2). A young man explained to
me that when he prayed he thought of God as an internal voice.
"He is a still small voice whose thoughts and reactions I feel within me." He was imagining God as the Word within himself. Perhaps you could think of God as the Word within you when you
pray.

Whether you imagine God as an internal voice or in the human
form of Jesus, you will need to avoid putting words into God's
mouth. He is not an actor reciting back to you the script you have
written for him, telling you the things you want to hear. To help
sidestep this problem, consider God as a confidant who will listen
and reflect on what you have to say, echoing your thoughts and
feelings like a non-directive counselor, but who will also challenge and encourage you to action through the power of the Holy
Spirit.

LETTERS TO GOD

Have you ever had the experience of thinking that you knew a friend until you received his first letter? A letter can give a different view of someone's personality. A person whom you would suspect to be humorless can turn out pages of witty prose, while a friend who is reticent about offering an opinion in a group can be quite forthright on paper.

Unlike a casual conversation, a letter is a permanent record of our thoughts and feelings, so we usually think twice before committing pen to paper. While I was studying in England, my future wife and I conducted a three year courtship by mail. Although we were separated by twelve thousand miles, we were able to remain close in spirit. We still enjoy corresponding when we are apart, as there is time to think about what we really want to say, knowing that the other partner is going to savor what is written.

People who have written letters to God confirm that this adds a new dimension to their prayer life. Instead of blurting out whatever comes to mind, they can develop more clearly their innermost thoughts and ideas. The procedure is the same as writing to anyone you dearly love. After opening with your greetings, spell out what is really on your mind. Don't feel that you have to write a massive epistle. There are postcards and telegrams too! One man who was not very articulate was advised by his minister to try the postcard technique. He painstakingly labored over each phrase, but the final result was worth the effort. He had succeeded in expressing exactly what he felt. Here is a sample:

Dear God,
I am glad you love me. I love you, too. I don't always

know how to say things but I feel them anyhow. Thank you for what you have done for me. Your true friend, Ron.

Another man poured out his anger in this letter:

Dear God:
If you love people as much as you say you do, why did you let those ten people die in that terrible fire yesterday? Bystanders heard their screams and were powerless to save them. God! What an awful way to go. How could you allow it to happen? I would do everything possible to help my children in a fire. If we're all your children, why didn't you do something?

After several more pages describing other tragedies, he told God he couldn't see any point in continuing their relationship. He had produced the proverbial "Dear John" letter, and like many such letters, it ended up being rewritten. In the first draft he vented his anger. Once he had calmed down, he started to reflect on Christ's sacrifice and love. He hadn't had his basic question answered, but he felt that he could trust again in God's love.

It might seem presumptuous to imagine how God would answer. Yet, we can learn about his will for us if we do attempt a reply. After you have written your letter to God, pray for the Holy Spirit's guidance in answering it. Don't feel you have to respond right away. It sometimes pays to wait several days. You must not assume that the answer you give is God's will, but it can provide insights. Be prepared for surprises. As she began a reply to her letter, one woman was startled to see God greeting her by name and thanking her for writing. She knew *in theory* that God loves and cares for each of us, but it really hadn't hit home until she saw it written out. A similar experience has been reported by some who could not accept God's forgiveness until they had seen it set down on paper.

Keep a file of your correspondence for future reference. It is a record of your relationship with God and how you understand him to be active in your life (see *Keeping in Touch*).

POETRY AND SONG

Once I heard a radio talk show where the topic was "expressing yourself in poetry." Within a few minutes, the switchboard was jammed with callers eager to share poems on the air. The art of poetry is obviously alive and well, and isn't the exclusive domain of Bohemian intellectuals.

You could be a budding poet yourself, so why not consider turning your talents to poems or hymns to God? Don't be shy. You are using verse to tell God how you feel, not applying for the position of poet laureate! All the devices of the poet are at your disposal: imagery, metaphor, simile, allusion, alliteration, assonance, irony, puns. You might choose to compose a sonnet, lyric, elegy, or limerick. Your poems don't have to rhyme; they could be free verse. Here is a non-rhyming poem I wrote on a retreat. While it might not be Wordsworth or Shakespeare, it is a prayer which I still find applicable.

> Lord, I am proud when I should be humble,
> Selfish when I should think of others,
> Uninterested when I should be concerned.
> I talk when I should listen,
> Condemn when I should understand,
> Grumble when I should give thanks,
> Envy when I should be satisfied,
> Betray when I should be trusting.
> You knock but I do not answer.
> Open the door of my heart
> That you may dwell within me forever. Amen.

Most children and teenagers go through a phase of expressing themselves in verse. Whenever I ask a church youth group to contribute prayers to a parish magazine, they inevitably write poetry, like these few lines submitted by Jocelyn Sherry:

> Your beauty surrounds me wherever I go.
> I praise you for all I see.
> Your guidance is with me, for I know
> That you will never leave me.

Your prayer poems can be turned into songs or hymns. It isn't necessary to compose original music. You could team up with someone who can, or write your own lyrics to an existing tune. If you plan to perform the music in public, check the copyright. Traditional favorites like "The Old Hundredth," "Jesu Joy of Man's Desiring," or "Faith of Our Fathers" are often set to alternative texts and have the advantage of being in the public domain. You could consider adding to the musical repertoire of your local church by contributing original verses for special occasions which may be neglected in the hymnal. Even if appropriate hymns are available, a setting of your own words at a wedding, baptism, anniversary, or funeral could make the ceremony more personal.

WHEN OTHERS SAY IT BETTER

We can always learn from studying the prayers of others. Their language and emphasis will be different from ours, and this can inspire our own prayers. When I first read Michel Quoist's *Prayers of Life,* I was struck by a prayer entitled "The Bald Head." It would never have occurred to me to make a hairless head the subject of a prayer. But Abbé Quoist, sitting behind a bald man at a boring lecture, associated this with Lk 21:18, "Not a hair of your head will be lost," and created a prayer on God's unique love. His reflections gave me a new perspective of what we can include in prayer. Malcolm Boyd has likewise shown us how we can draw on everyday experience. His social commentary prayers in *Are You Running with Me, Jesus?* include reflections on films, sexual freedom, and an empty house, as well as loneliness and racial attitudes.

Some people are gifted in writing prayers. They can express feelings to God much better than we can. Most of us never tire of re-reading the well-known prayers, such as the prayer for peace attributed to St. Francis of Assisi (see *The Close Up*), or this one by St. Ignatius of Loyola:

> Teach us, good Lord, to serve thee as thou deservest:
> To give and not to count the cost;
> To fight and not to heed the wounds;
> To toil and not to seek for rest;
> To labor and not to ask for any reward
> Save that of knowing that we do thy will.

Or take this popular example from the *Old Sarum Primer:*

> God be in my head,
>   And in my understanding;
> God be in my eyes,
>   And in my looking;
> God be in my mouth,
>   And in my speaking;
> God be in my heart,
>   And in my thinking;
> God be at my end,
>   And at my departing.

You might consider making personal additions or adapting existing prayers. In the above example, you could add:

> God be in my ears,
>   And in my listening;
> God be in my hands,
>   And in my working.

There are many inspired prayers in print, and most of us have favorites. I particularly like the sonnet "Batter my heart, three person'd God" by John Donne, the psalms, and many of the prayers of Thomas à Kempis in *The Imitation of Christ.* You will have your own preferences but don't limit yourself to these. If you expose yourself to a wide range of writers, their prayers will help to balance the content of your own. There are plenty of published collections, including liturgical prayer books and missals. Some of the hymns we sing make good prayers, while the Bible, especially the psalter and John's Gospel, is another rich source.

Other people's prayers can help in times of spiritual dryness. They can give you a wealth of material to fall back on when you are stuck for words. For this reason, Christians of some traditions lay great emphasis on memorized prayers. When you use someone else's prayer, take it slowly. Don't rush. We have all heard those charge-of-the-light-brigade recitations when no one has time to pause or reflect. Think about the meaning of the words. Let them become *your* words.

SECTION IV

Traditional Forms of Prayer

LEARNING TO MEDITATE

Whenever my father stretched out on the sofa for forty winks, he would never admit to being asleep. He always insisted he was meditating. We were supposed to believe that he had been pondering some deep, philosophical issue. When my father, on the other hand, caught me daydreaming instead of getting on with the job, I would offer him the same explanation. Needless to say, the term "meditation" became a standard family joke.

But meditation needn't be unproductive. Taking time out to reflect on a subject can provide worthwhile insights. We can use meditation as a prayer technique to increase our awareness of God and discover his will for us.

A number of spiritual writers have given us suggestions on how this can be done. The methods can be carefully structured such as those of St. Ignatius of Loyola, St. Francis de Sales, and the Sulpician school, or they can be loosely structured—for instance, a simple reflection on nature, or a free association. You may choose to meditate on a concrete object, such as a seed, flower, or a stained glass window, a story from the Scriptures or the lives of the saints, or more abstract concepts like truth, love, sacrifice, or God's mercy.

At the simplest level, a prayer meditation might be a free association. Start with a theological theme and let your mind flow in an uninterrupted stream of consciousness. If your subject is the second commandment against worshiping graven images (Ex 20:4), your associations might flow like this: graven images . . . golden calf . . . Moses on the mountain . . . tablets . . . Ten Commandments . . . Cecil B. De Mille extravaganza . . . Hollywood commercialization of God . . . At this point you might go off on a tangent and think about the economy, inflation, your own bank account and the bills that are due, whether you should ask for a raise, or whether it would be beneficial to belong to a select club for business contacts. Our digressions usually lead to what is uppermost in our minds, so treat these detours as an exercise in self-discovery. But don't spend too long on these side excursions. Return to the original topic and begin your associations again. If you do this you might well view your digressions in a new light. When you reflect on your financial preoccupations in terms of the graven image, your associations might now include the ways in which your material goals stand between you and God.

This last technique is a relatively unstructured form of meditation and can frequently become little more than daydreaming. To avoid this most meditation techniques provide a framework which gives direction and purpose to the meditation. Most methods have the following three parts in common: preparation, consideration of the chosen topic, and resolution, in which a promise is made to God to carry out a specific action.

Here is a general more structured meditation technique. Begin by picking a theme—a passage from Scripture, the lives of the saints, the words of a well-known prayer, an object from nature, one of the sacraments, or a mystery of faith. Think carefully about the topic you choose, making sure that you understand it, and that it will give you some insights into how you might live a fuller Christian life. If you select the incarnation or Christ's passion and want to go beyond a superficial level, be prepared to allot long periods of time, or break up the subject into installments.

After your preparation (see *Making Contact*), consider the topic you have decided upon in light of the following questions:

1. What are the facts? What do I know about it?
2. What does it mean? To me? To others?
3. What does God want me to do about it?

Suppose you settle on the topic of baptism. First, think about what is taking place from the standpoint of the candidate, the officiant, the sponsors, and the congregation. Then consider the water and what it symbolizes—the cleansing of sin, renewing of life in Christ, the entering of the Holy Spirit, and joining the Church. Perhaps your Church anoints with holy oil as well. When you reflect on what baptism means to you, recall your own, or if you were too young to remember, think about the promises that were made on your behalf. Your thoughts could turn to your own godchildren or the people recently admitted to your congregation. As a resolution, you might thank God that you are part of his Church and for all the benefits you have received as a member of the body of Christ, or maybe raise the question of your own commitment to the faith. Perhaps your meditation will motivate you to write, telephone, or visit your godchildren. You might also seek ways to be more welcoming to new members of your parish. Try to carry out your intentions as soon as possible. Otherwise, they might end up like so many New Year's resolutions!

Most of the well-known meditation procedures are elaborations on this basic format. Some of these techniques, such as The Time Machine and The Salesian Devotion, are suitable for an imaginative re-creation of a scene in all its vividness. The traditional Dominican rosary is a controlled means of reflecting on fifteen scenes from the life of Jesus and his Mother, while The Close-Up is designed for detailed examination of a text. The Nature Study deals with God's creation as well as objects we have made, whereas the Sulpician Approach emphasizes the heart as well as the mind.

In much of the literature on spirituality, you will find that meditation and contemplation are used interchangeably, and to add to the confusion, Asian writers also refer to their methods as meditation. But whatever terms are used, a distinction can be drawn between the more rational and imaginative discursive process which I have described here as meditation, and the imageless inner stillness, or resting in God, of the contemplative.

THE TIME MACHINE

In his famous short novel, *The Time Machine*, H. G. Wells gives a fictional account of journeys into the fourth dimension. His central character, The Time Traveller, had invented a way of transporting himself into the past or future. Ever since this story appeared, the concept of breaking the time barrier has gripped our imagination. Perhaps you have dreamed of meeting Cleopatra, debating with Aristotle, asking Shakespeare whether he wrote *Hamlet*, attending the premiere performance of Handel's *Messiah*, or watching the trial and crucifixion of Jesus of Nazareth.

Though science has yet to provide us with a time machine, our imagination can be a useful tool to recreate the past or speculate on the future. In your meditations, you can imagine yourself as a participant or observer of a scene from the Bible or lives of the saints. It is like creating a movie in your mind: you can use your imagination to set the scene, characters, and dialogue.

Choose a story which you can visualize, preferably an action scene, such as Jesus driving out the money changers from the temple, the feeding of the five thousand, the wedding at Cana, the martyrdom of St. Stephen, St. Paul's shipwreck on Malta, or a parable such as the Good Samaritan. Once you have decided on a subject, read the passage several times so that you are thoroughly familiar with it. Then select the role you are to play. If you choose to identify with the victim in the narrative of the Good Samaritan (Lk 10:29f), imagine yourself on the dusty road from Jerusalem to Jericho. How do you feel? Hot? Tired? What are you thinking about? In one of my meditations, this is how I began to picture the scene.

> The heat was stifling and I was anxious to get back to Jericho. I had heard stories of robbers along the route and was praying my luck would hold. There were still many miles to go as I moved into a canyon. "What the . . . !" I gasped, as a surge of fear raced up my spine. Two men with knives drawn had sprung out from behind the rocks. I muttered to myself, "There's not a Roman soldier around when you need one." When I turned to escape, I found two more armed men behind me. I was trapped. "They are going to kill me! Lord, have mercy!" I saw stars before my eyes. When I awoke, my head ached. Flies were crawling on my face, but I couldn't brush them away. After a while, I heard someone coming down the road and tried to make a sound to attract his attention. He paused for a moment, then went on his way. The pain became more intense. They must have beaten me badly. Someone else approached . . .

There is no need to be scrupulous about historical accuracy. Does it really matter if you pictured green pastures in this arid region of Palestine or an asphalt road in the first century? After all, the purpose of this exercise is to come to a deeper appreciation of the Gospel message and its implications for you.

St. Ignatius of Loyola (1491–1556) is credited with popularizing this you-are-there technique. In his *Spiritual Exercises,* he suggested recreating the scene in our imagination, then considering the main points of the story, what they mean to us, and how we can act on them.

What are the most striking points of the story as you visualize it? In the Good Samaritan, they might be the irony of being helped by a despised ethnic minority and the hypocrisy of the respected religious figures who turned away. Don't forget to include your feelings. Were you angry about being an innocent victim, rejected, and having to accept charity? Or were you grateful that one person cared?

After you have recalled the main points, spend a few minutes thinking about how they apply to you. Perhaps you could ask yourself these questions: What racial prejudices do I have? Do I reject other people in need, like the lonely neighbor who wanted to talk with me? Or the senile terminally ill patient in a nursing home? Or the tramps, migrant workers, and others regarded as being at the bottom of the social ladder? Then ask yourself if you really want to help these people. What have you already done for them, and what more could you do?

Once you have thought about how the story relates to you, ask yourself what you intend to do about it. Should I learn more about the customs and culture of the ethnic group that I am biased against? Could I help recent immigrants learn my language? When can I invite my neighbor over for coffee? Perhaps you could see a friend in the hospital, lend a hand at a local emergency shelter, or offer your skills in some other way. Pray for God's guidance in forming specific resolutions and in carrying them out.

You might care to use The Time Machine to test the practicality of your resolutions by imagining their consequences. Can you see yourself as a regular visitor to the convalescent home? Could you be a close friend to the lonely neighbor? You might envision yourself performing heroic good deeds, but in practice never carrying out your fine intentions. The aim of the meditation is to encourage you to live the Gospel in practical terms, not to become like H. G. Wells' Time Traveller who never returned to the present.

REFLECTING ON NATURE

"I have only to look at a flower, a bird in flight, or think about the intricacies of the human body to know that God is all around me." How often have you heard phrases like these? Perhaps you have uttered them yourself. When we pause to reflect on nature—the ocean's immensity and changing moods, the vastness of the galaxies, the miracle of new life, or even the ecological role of the mosquito—we can feel overwhelmed by the complex interrelationships of the natural scheme. This fascination with nature can be the basis of a meditation which can lead to an awareness of God's presence and our place in his creation.

Choose an object you know something about and can examine in detail—a leaf, flower, feather, shell, rock, vegetable, fruit, or seed. Observe it closely. Shut your eyes and touch it. Is it rough or smooth, hard or soft, rigid or pliable? Does it have a smell or make any sounds? Now open your eyes and take a good look at it from different angles. What shape and colors does it have? What are its component parts and how are they arranged? Learn as much as you can about the object from your own senses before considering its significance and the symbolic associations it might evoke.

If you decide to meditate on a stalk of wheat, feel the kernels, noting the texture, firmness, color, and shape. Split one or two of them and look at the grains inside. When you have made your observations, turn your attention to its various functions. What part does it play in the ecological chain? Does it provide food or contribute to the nitrogen or carbon cycles? In the case of the wheat, it is both food and seed. After you have gained an appreciation of its place in the natural order, thank God for his creation, and ask for direction in using wisely all that he has given us.

The next step is to consider possible symbolic associations. In the parable of the sower (Mk 4:3f), Jesus gives us an example of how an analogy can be drawn from nature. The seed symbolizes the word, and the seeds that grow to maturity represent those of us who hear the word and act on it. Perhaps you will find a lesson like this in nature. A three-leaf clover led St. Patrick to reflect on the Holy Trinity, a rock might bring to mind St. Peter and the Church, while the meditation on the wheat could raise thoughts on "our daily bread" and the Eucharist.

In a meditation class, a divorced man who fixed his attention on a leaf felt that the difference between its rough and smooth sides could be a comment on his attitude to life since he had focused almost totally on the rough side—domestic turmoil and the trauma of separation—to the exclusion of the positive or smooth side of his life—his children, close friends, good health, and a rewarding career. A teenager, concentrating on a dandelion, at first related the plainness of the flower to her own lack of beauty. But after looking more closely, she realized that, like the flower with its many petals, she possessed many talents and special qualities, and as it was a cheerful yellow color, she too should be glad in her own unique attributes.

Pray that the Holy Spirit will show you what you can learn from nature. But don't force tenuous or bizarre associations. The symbolism could become far-fetched. If nothing figurative readily comes to mind, just appreciate God's creation and give thanks.

Sometimes the object itself will suggest a course of action. After examining the wheat and thinking of it as basic food, you might be led to consider the hungry and deprived, who constitute the majority of the world's population, and investigate what contributions you could make. A meditation on a pine cone might prompt you to see what could be done to stop destruction of park lands. You might become active in a conservation group, or plant a tree in your own backyard.

At other times your course of action will be determined by the symbolic associations you have made. In the meditation class, the man who found an analogy for his divorce when he looked at the rough and smooth sides of a leaf resolved to thank God for the good things that happened each day. The resolution of the teenager who looked on herself as a Plain Jane, on the other hand, was to make a note of three positive qualities every day for a week, to thank God for them, and ask him how she could strengthen her good qualities and use them in his service.

This meditation technique can also be extended to tools, machinery, buildings, and other inanimate objects. The procedure is the same. A hoe or a rake could lead you to thoughts about weeding a garden, and by extension to cultivating your spiritual life. A machine might impress you with the intricacy of its design, and move you to reflect on the complexity of human beings and God's design for us, while a church building might raise questions about your involvement with the Christian community and the active part you could play as a member of God's family.

THE ROSARY

The rosary is undoubtedly the most popular of all meditation techniques. Described by Pope Paul VI as "a Gospel prayer, centered on the mystery of the redemptive incarnation," and by Pius XII as "the compendium of the entire Gospel," it highlights the key events in the life of Jesus and his mother.

This devotion grew out of the monastic practice of reciting the one hundred and fifty psalms. While some of the monks knew them all by heart and a few could read them, the rest had to substitute an equivalent number of rote prayers, usually one hundred and fifty Our Fathers or Hail Marys, a custom that was adopted by the laity. For this reason, the rosary became known as "The People's Psalter." Since it was easy to lose count of the prayers, beads and other devices came into use. Interestingly, the word bead comes from "bede," which in Middle English meant a prayer. The rosary gradually evolved from a simple recitation of rote prayers to a more complex combination of meditation and memorized prayer. Although the modern rosary is attributed to St. Dominic (1170–1221), and is often referred to as the Dominican rosary, it wasn't until the sixteenth century that it was established in its present form.

Unlike most other meditation methods which leave the choice of subject matter open, the rosary consists of fifteen prescribed scenes from the life of Jesus and Mary. These scenes or mysteries are divided into three groups of five meditations. The first five, known as the *Joyful Mysteries,* include:

1. *Annunciation*	The angel Gabriel announces to the Virgin Mary that she will bear a son to be named Jesus (Lk 1:26).
2. *Visitation*	Mary visits her cousin Elizabeth before John the Baptist's birth (Lk 1:41f).
3. *Nativity*	The Christ Child is born in Bethlehem (Lk 2:1).
4. *Presentation*	Mary goes to the temple for purification and Jesus is consecrated to God (Lk 2:22–24).
5. *Finding Jesus in the Temple*	The twelve year old Jesus astounds the doctors of the law (Lk 2:41f).

The *Sorrowful Mysteries* are centered around Jesus' passion:

6. *Agony in the Garden*	Jesus sweats in trepidation as he submits to his Father's will (Mk 14:32f).
7. *Scourging at the Pillar*	Jesus is whipped (Jn 19:1).
8. *Crowning with Thorns*	Jesus' kingship is mocked (Mt 27:28f).
9. *Carrying the Cross*	Jesus makes his way to Golgotha (Jn 19:17).
10. *Crucifixion*	Jesus dies on the cross for our sins (Lk 23:46).

The last group, the *Glorious Mysteries,* include:

11. *Resurrection*	Jesus rises from the dead (Mk 16:6).
12. *Ascension*	Jesus goes to be with his Father (Mk 16:19).
13. *Descent of the Holy Spirit*	At Pentecost the disciples receive the Holy Spirit (Acts 2:4).

| 14. *Assumption* | Mary is received into heaven (Rev 12:1f). |
| 15. *Coronation* | Mary is crowned Queen of Heaven. |

It is customary to pray only one set of five mysteries at a time. Unless your rosary is an oversize model, you will have to go around it three times to pray all fifteen mysteries.

You can meditate on these mysteries in any number of ways. You might imagine the scene from the standpoint of Jesus, his mother, or yourself as an observer (see *Time Machine*). Alternatively, you could linger on one specific aspect of the mystery, such as joy at the coming of the Christ Child, or Christ's forgiveness from the cross. Or you may even draw some practical resolution from the meditation, such as your own need to be obedient to God, like Jesus in the Garden of Gethsemane.

However you focus on the mysteries, your meditation should occupy the foreground while your vocal prayers—the Lord's Prayer, Hail Mary, and Gloria Patri—said silently or aloud, remain in the background.

At first it will seem like trying to rub your stomach and pat your head at the same time, but after practice, the verbal prayers will become automatic.

The Hail Mary is said this way:

> Hail Mary, full of grace,
> > the Lord is with thee;
> blessed art thou amongst women,
> > and blessed is the fruit of thy womb, Jesus.
> Holy Mary, Mother of God,
> > pray for us sinners,
> now and at the hour of our death. Amen.

The Gloria Patri usually takes this form:

> Glory be to the Father, and to the Son, and to the Holy Ghost. As it was in the beginning, is now, and ever shall be, world without end. Amen.

You don't need beads to pray the rosary, but it frees your mind for the meditations if you have a means of keeping track of the vocal prayers. Most rosaries are divided into five sets of ten Hail Mary beads with a single Our Father bead in between. These are arranged in a circle, and constitute the main body of the rosary. An appendage, which includes the crucifix and five additional beads, is reserved for preparatory prayers.

To pray the rosary, begin at the crucifix and repeat the Apostles' Creed:

> I believe in God the Father Almighty, maker of heaven and
>   earth:
> And in Jesus Christ his only Son our Lord,
> Who was conceived by the Holy Ghost,
> Born of the Virgin Mary,
> Suffered under Pontius Pilate,
> Was crucified, died, and was buried:
> He descended into hell;
> The third day he rose again from the dead;
> He ascended into heaven,
> And sitteth at the right hand of God the Father Almighty;
> From thence he shall come to judge the quick and the
>   dead.
>
> I believe in the Holy Ghost; the holy catholic Church;
> the communion of saints; the forgiveness of sins; the
> resurrection of the body, and life everlasting.
> Amen.

Now proceed to the first bead, and say the Lord's Prayer. On the next three beads—which according to different traditions symbolize either the Holy Trinity or faith, hope, and charity—pray three Hail Marys and follow this with a Gloria Patri. At this point, you might prefer to insert your special requests to God before going on to the mysteries. After you have made your petitions, announce the first mystery, and describe it to yourself in a few words. While you are meditating on its meaning, repeat the Lord's Prayer on the fifth bead. Continue your reflections as you pray the Hail Mary ten times through the next ten beads, finishing the decade with a Gloria Patri. Then announce the second

Rosary

mystery, say the Lord's Prayer on the next Our Father bead, and continue the same procedure throughout the rest of the rosary.

When the rosary is prayed out loud in a group, it is customary to add Marian prayers, such as Hail Holy Queen or the Memorare, at the conclusion of the five decades. It is also usual, especially when the rosary is prayed individually, to end with a general thanksgiving to God.

Although the rosary is a structured meditation, there is room for flexibility. Sometimes you may wish to pray the five decades using just one or two of the mysteries. At other times you may want to concentrate on the verbal prayers and make them the subject of your meditation, or you might be drawn toward affective prayer or contemplation. If you find it difficult to meditate and recite vocal prayers simultaneously, you can always say these prayers after you have meditated on the mystery.

Although the Dominican rosary is the most common, there are many others. Some are variations, like the seven decade Franciscan crown which extends the number of joyful mysteries, or the chaplet of St. Joseph which retains all fifteen mysteries but reduces the number of vocal prayers. Other rosaries emphasize special themes, such as the seven sorrows of Our Lady, the thirteen virtues of St. Anthony, the Holy Spirit, the Sacred Heart of Jesus, Blessed Sacrament, or the Stations of the Cross. There are multitudes of devotions, most of them dating from the nineteenth century.

Of the societies that promote the rosary, the Confraternity of the Holy Rosary, the Legion of Mary, and the Rosary League are active within the Roman Catholic Church, while the Living Rosary of Our Lady and St. Dominic encourage the practice among Anglicans. Contact your local diocesan office for further information.

Many Protestants have shied away from the rosary because of its emphasis on Mary, although in recent years some Protestant clergy have expressed the need for a more disciplined form of meditation and have adapted the rosary. One way of doing this is to reduce the mysteries to a basic five: the Nativity, Agony in the Garden, Crucifixion, Resurrection, and the Descent of the Holy Spirit at Pentecost. You could also choose other scriptural material such as Jesus' baptism, the temptation of the wilderness, recruiting of the disciples, the triumphant entry into Jerusalem, the Last Supper, and the Seven Last Words from the cross. Alternative verbal prayers could include the Jesus Prayer, or the Sanctus:

Holy, holy, holy, Lord God of Hosts;
Heaven and earth are full of thy Glory;
Glory be to thee, O Lord Most High.

Another possibility is this verse from Psalm 19:

Let the words of my mouth and the meditation of my heart be acceptable in thy sight, O Lord, my rock and my redeemer.

Or consider the King James Version of John 3:16:

> For God so loved the world, that he gave his only begotten Son, that whosoever believeth in him should not perish, but have everlasting life.

There are numerous possibilities.

Rosary beads have been fashioned of precious stones and metals, wood, ivory, rose petals, and olive pits. You don't have to use the commercially made variety. You could make your own. A knotted string or some other counting device—even your ten fingers—can serve as a tactile aid to making your meditations more systematic and your prayer life more disciplined.

THE CLOSE-UP

"I need time for it all to sink in," first-time visitors have remarked after a church service. It is a comment that those of us who attend regularly could take to heart—especially when it comes to the familiar prayers like the Lord's Prayer, Gloria in Excelsis, Anima Christi, Ave Maria, and the Magnificat, which are repeated so often. In the same way that the photographer helps us to appreciate the overview of a scene by focusing on the close-ups, we can come to a fuller understanding of these prayers when we examine them in detail—word by word or a phrase at a time.

Begin by selecting a prayer, the creeds, parts of the liturgy, or scriptural passages like the Beatitudes and the Ten Commandments. After you have chosen a text, say it through several times so that you are familiar with it as a whole. Then break it down into manageable segments. Most prayers, like St. Francis' "Lord, make me an instrument of your peace," lend themselves to a phrase by phrase analysis, while the Jesus Prayer and the Lord's Prayer can be viewed microscopically, a word or two at a time. Start with the first word or phrase. Let the associations flow. Then move on to the second word or phrase. One woman reported to me that she never before appreciated the first word of the Lord's Prayer until she began to meditate on the implications of the "our" of Our Father. "It brought home to me," she said, "that this was not just *my* Father, but *our* Father. He belongs to us all. Until then, I had been treating him as though I were an only child."

This single word was enough to occupy her meditation. When St. Ignatius recommended this technique, he advised that the meditator should reflect on a word "as long as he finds meanings, comparisons, relish, and consolation in the consideration of it" (*Spiritual Exercises*, Fourth Week).

In this popular prayer attributed to St. Francis of Assisi, each phrase can easily become the subject of a meditation:

> Lord, make me an instrument of your peace.
> Where there is hatred, let me sow love;
> Where there is injury, pardon;
> Where there is doubt, faith;
> Where there is despair, hope;
> Where there is darkness, light;
> Where there is sadness, joy.

> O Divine Master, grant that I may seek not so much to be consoled as to console; to be understood as to understand; to be loved as to love; for it is in giving that we receive; it is in pardoning that we are pardoned; and it is in dying that we are born to eternal life. Amen.

As you review each phrase, you could think of the instances of hatred, injury, and doubt on a global or local level, and practical ways to extend love, offer pardon, or increase faith. Don't feel that you must complete the prayer all in one session. You might prefer to spread the material over several days or weeks. The next time you return to the prayer, begin by repeating it over in its entirety before resuming your meditation.

SALESIAN DEVOTION

"It may be that you don't know how to pray mentally . . . for unfortunately this is something that few people in our time know how to do," wrote the French bishop, St. Francis de Sales (1567–1622) in his *Introduction to the Devout Life* (pp. 83–84). He decided to remedy this situation by offering one of the first practical prayer guides for the laity. It included a simply structured meditation technique which he divided into preparation, considerations of the chosen subject, affections and resolutions, and conclusion and spiritual bouquet.

Preparation

After you have chosen a suitable topic, such as a mystery of faith or a Gospel theme, begin your meditation by placing yourself in the presence of God, using one of these four ways:

- Recognize that God is everywhere and is present in all things.
- Remember that God is especially present "in your heart and in the very center of your spirit" (p. 85).
- Imagine Jesus looking down from heaven while you are at prayer.
- Imagine that Jesus is actually present with you, as you would imagine a friend present.

St. Francis advises not to put these ways into practice all at once, "but only one at a time and that briefly and simply" (p. 86).

In the second part of the preparation, ask for God's assistance "in order to serve and adore him properly in this meditation" (p. 86).

St. Francis also suggests that you could ask for guidance from
your guardian angel or else a saint. Your saint might be the Virgin
Mary if you are meditating on the nativity, or St. John or Mary
Magdalene if you have selected the crucifixion.

The final part of the preparation is to visualize the mystery or
Gospel scene as if it were taking place before your eyes (see *Time
Machine*). This part is not essential to the meditation, and is not
recommended for abstract themes like God's greatness or the
purpose of our creation.

Considerations

After your preparation, the next stage is to select one or two
points from the topic of your meditation and reflect on their
meaning. If you choose the stoning of St. Stephen (Acts 7:55f), for
instance, you could highlight the way this martyr was prepared to
go to his death while forgiving his persecutors. If you find enough
substance in just one point, remain with it, but don't feel obliged
to squeeze your subject dry. St. Francis suggests that we "imitate
the bees, who do not leave a flower as long as they can extract
any honey out of it. But if you do not come on anything that ap-
peals to you after you have examined and tried it out for a while,
then go on to another, but proceed calmly and simply in this matter and do not rush yourself" (p. 88).

Affections and Resolutions

The meditation should produce feelings of love for God and a desire to do his will. But you will need to turn these feelings into
specific resolutions. In the example of St. Stephen, you could try
to imitate him by pardoning and reconciling yourself with those
who have made disparaging remarks about your beliefs or even
discriminated against you because of your faith.

Conclusion and Spiritual Bouquet

In concluding your meditation, thank God for what you have
learned and for the resolutions he has given you. Then offer to
him your desire to carry out the resolutions and ask him to bless

them. St. Francis de Sales suggests at this point praying for the Church, clergy, relatives, friends, and others who need our intercessions, after which you could pray the Lord's Prayer or the Hail Mary. Finally, choose a few of the points you have been meditating on to savor throughout the day. St. Francis calls this the "spiritual bouquet": "People who have been walking about in a beautiful garden," he says, "do not like to leave without gathering in their hands four or five flowers to smell and keep for the rest of the day. In the same way, when our soul has carefully considered by meditation a certain mystery we should select one, two, or three points that we liked best and that are most adapted to our improvement, think frequently about them, and smell them spiritually during the rest of the day" (p. 90).

SULPICIAN APPROACH

"To have Jesus before the eyes, in the heart, and in the hands: that is the whole Christian life." This comment of Fr. Louis Tronson (1622–1700) would summarize the essence of the Sulpician method of meditation, which originated with Cardinal de Bérulle and Fr. Jean-Jacques Olier, who founded the Society of St. Sulpice in Paris in 1641.

The heart of the Sulpician approach is adoring Christ and his virtues, making these virtues our own, and trying to live by them—adoration, communion, and cooperation. Fr. Tronson added some supplementary material—preparation, considerations, and self-examination, as well as a conclusion. It is his version that is outlined here with slight modifications, since the original text was intended for seminarians.

Preparation

Ideally, you should begin your preparation the night before. Select one of Jesus' virtues—humility, compassion, obedience, love, mercy. To give you inspiration, you might want to refer to relevant passages in the Gospels. Keep the topic in mind as you go to sleep, and plan to do your meditation soon after rising.

When you are ready to meditate, place yourself in the Lord's presence (see *Salesian Devotion*), recognizing before him your own unworthiness and dependence. Then call upon the Holy Spirit to guide you. You could also pray the *Veni Creator Spiritus*, the complete text of which can be found in many prayer books and hymnals, and which begins:

Come, Holy Ghost, our souls inspire,
And lighten with celestial fire,
Thou the anointing Spirit art,
Who dost thy sevenfold gifts impart.

Body of the Prayer/Meditation

Adoration: Jesus before your eyes.
Think about the subject in a general way, as a backdrop to enable you to dwell on the incarnate Lord. If you choose Jesus' humility, don't get sidetracked with reconstructing what took place at the Last Supper (Jn 13:1f), why Jesus chose to wash the feet of his disciples, what kind of basin he used, where he got the water from, or the symbolic significance of Peter's comments. Instead offer him your feelings of adoration, admiration, praise, love, joy, and gratitude.

Communion: Jesus in your heart.
After you have adored this virtue in Jesus, consider your own deficiency, and then open your heart to let the virtue become part of you. Fr. Tronson compared this with receiving the Communion host. "As we commune with the body of our Lord when we open the mouth and receive him," he said, "so we commune with his virtues and his spirit when opening the mouth of our soul; we receive him in our heart."

Cooperation: Jesus in your hands.
Having received the virtue in your heart, make a specific resolution to carry this out in your life. You are cooperating with God in putting this virtue into practice. Set yourself realistic goals, and go about fulfilling them as soon as you can.

Conclusion

Thank God for the graces you have received during your meditation, and ask forgiveness for any lack of attention or half-heartedness. Ask him to bless your resolutions, then select a thought to carry with you during the rest of the day as a *spiritual bouquet.*

CONTEMPLATION

Sometimes when I am telling my wife how much I care for her, she will interrupt and say, "Shhh, you don't have to say anything. Let's just be still and enjoy the moment together." We have reached a point where it is enough just to be with each other and share feelings of warmth and tenderness in silent communion. Words would break the spell.

This can also happen in our relationship with God. We can feel that he is so close, within and about us, that we no longer need to reach out with words. When this occurs, why not be silent and savor the moment? In theological language, you could transcend the symbols to approach the reality, so that love meets love. Shut out all thoughts and images, and remain quietly in God's presence, absorbing and reflecting his love. In the words of St. John of the Cross, you could "remain alone in loving awareness of God, without particular considerations, in interior peace and quiet repose, and without the acts and exercises . . . of the intellect, memory and will" (*Ascent of Mount Carmel*, II:13). The experience may last only a few moments, but it could soon develop into longer periods.

You might find that once you have placed yourself in the presence of God you are drawn even closer to him. The warm-up procedure, described in *Making Contact*, can move us toward contemplation, as it is a way of eliminating distractions and placing ourselves in God's presence. I have frequently used this type of preparation with parish groups as a lead into five and ten minute periods of contemplation, and despite some writers who have regarded it as an advanced form of prayer, I have been pleasantly surprised at the positive reaction. Many pre-teens and teenagers have come up to me afterward with comments like: "What a fabulous way to pray! I never know what to say to God anyway, but this time I felt so relaxed and warm in his love." With experience, contemplation will come more easily—not only at scheduled prayer times but throughout the day. Be patient. Don't force contemplation, but remain trusting, allowing nothing to disturb your inner stillness.

If you find your attention wandering, it can help to have a single short word that will enable you to center again on God. The anonymous fourteenth century author of *The Cloud of Unknowing* advises us: "A one-syllable word like 'God' or 'love' is best. But choose one that is meaningful to you. Then fix it in your mind so that it will remain there come what may" (p. 56). Return to the centering word whenever you need to refocus on God. If you find you are becoming restless during contemplation, and the centering word doesn't help, then try some other form of prayer. It is important to stay fluid.

You might prefer to use the Jesus Prayer (or some other Christian mantra) as a vehicle for contemplation. The constant repetition of the words—*Lord Jesus Christ, Son of God, have mercy on me a sinner*—acts as a centrifugal force to draw you back to the divine without intruding on interior silence.

Although contemplation is primarily a silent resting in the Lord, there will be occasions when you will be so overwhelmed with his love that you will long to express these feelings. When two lovers are together, they often declare their love by repeating simple endearments like "I love you" or "You mean everything to me." To an outsider the words might appear trite and extravagant, while to the couple they are attempts to express their devotion. You could express your love to God in the same way.

Let your adoration spill out in short endearments or "aspirations" as they are sometimes called. Don't hold back. Tell God what is in your heart (see *Cries to God*). St. Francis of Assisi exclaimed, "My God and my all," while St. Thérèse of Lisieux (1873–1897) phrased her sentiments more passionately: "O my Jesus, draw me into the fires of your love, and unite me so closely to yourself that you may live and act in me." In this century, Pope John XXIII cried, "O my God, may my only reward be—your mercy!" Endearments such as these will often rise spontaneously from the heart throughout the day, not just during your set time of prayer.

As contemplation is a unique, individual experience, an open style of prayer with little structure done in solitude, it could lead to a number of problems. For this reason, it is vital to have spiritual guidance (see *Spiritual Director*). Sometimes beginners look upon contemplation as an elite form of prayer and attempt to plunge into it without sufficient preparation or an adequate understanding of what is involved. Contemplation should flow out of an appreciation of God through study, meditation, verbal prayer, self-examination, humility, and living the faith. Beginners can also become impatient with the extended periods of stillness, or have unrealistic expectations of spectacular revelations. Rarely, it may lead to visions or hallucinations.

Contemplation has often been viewed as spiritual escapism, retreating into oneself in a private relationship with God, to the exclusion of the rest of the world. But if contemplation leads us to be filled with God's love, this should surely radiate through us to others and touch their lives.

THE MYSTICAL WAY

The mystical way has often been shrouded in mystery. It has been thought of in terms of the occult, sensational supernatural phenomena, visions, or an ethereal spirituality—beyond our understanding and outside the mainstream of our faith. Yet Christian mysticism plays a very significant part in our Christian prayer heritage. Some mystics—St. Teresa of Avila, St. John of the Cross, and Juliana of Norwich, for example—had the ability or the gift to cultivate an in-depth relationship with God through the contemplative life, attaining a special state of union which few of us will approach. If we can draw any distinction between the mystic and the contemplative, it would be a matter of intensity, the union with God being described as the mystical experience. A number of other mystics have also written about their prayer experiences, and to understand something of the paths they have taken, their recommendations for us, and their own poetic descriptions of union with God, it is well worth studying some of their works.

One of the most succinct accounts is found in *The Stairway of Perfection* by Walter Hilton, a fourteenth century English mystic. He divides the development of the contemplative life into three stages. The first is our knowledge of God, which comes through study and meditation. The second stage is mainly one of affection. At the lower level this takes the form of an outpouring of love for all that God has done for us. These feelings, he says, are from God and will come and go, as the Lord wills. The higher level of this second stage comes after we have been fully reconciled to God and have attained physical and inner stillness. Once this point has been reached, nothing should please us more, Walter

Hilton says, than to sit still and "continuously praise God and think about our Lord" (p. 69). He also adds that centering words such as the name of Jesus, the Our Father, and other traditional prayers and hymns of the Church will increase our affections for God and strengthen us against sin and distractions.

Finally, the contemplative is able to go beyond physical surroundings, thoughts, and feelings to combine knowledge of God and affection for him:

> Then, by the grace of the Holy Spirit the soul is illuminated in understanding, so that it sees the essential Truth which is God, and spiritual things. This illumination is so perfectly accompanied by a soft, sweet burning love in Him that the soul, for the time being, is made one with God and conformed to the image of the Trinity by this ravishing love (*The Stairway of Perfection*, pp. 70–71).

One of the greatest of all mystical writers is St. John of the Cross (1542–1591). He describes through poems and commentaries the process of divine union as a journey through a dark night. In *The Ascent of Mount Carmel*, he emphasizes the need to cast aside bodily pleasures and desires, what he calls the *night of sense*, as well as emptying ourselves of spiritual feelings and thoughts—the *night of the spirit.* He reminds us of what Jesus said: "If anyone wants to be a follower of mine, let him renounce himself and take up his cross and follow me" (Mk 8:34), and tells us that we must rely on *dark faith,* knowing not where the journey will lead:

> Like a blind man he must lean on dark faith, accept it for his guide and light, and rest on nothing of what he understands, tastes, feels, or imagines. All these perceptions are a darkness that will lead him astray. Faith lies beyond all this understanding, taste, feeling, and imagining. If he does not blind himself in these things and abide in total darkness, he will not reach what is greater—the teaching of faith (*The Ascent of Mount Carmel*, II:4:2).

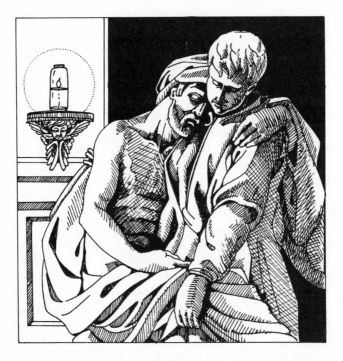

In *The Dark Night of the Soul,* he explains that this darkness is a painful time of apprehension and despair, when God is purifying us so that we can be made ready for a new life in union with him. In *The Spiritual Canticle* and *The Living Flame of Love,* he depicts the purified soul illuminated and inflamed with divine love, and uses the images of betrothal and marriage to illustrate the mystical union that is possible between God and ourselves.

> This spiritual marriage is incomparably greater than the spiritual espousal, for it is total transformation in the Beloved in which each renders the entire possession of self to the other with a certain consummation of the union of love. The soul thereby becomes divine, becomes God through participation, insofar as is possible in this life. . . . It is accordingly the highest state attainable in this life (*The Spiritual Canticle,* 22:3).

St. Teresa of Avila (1515–1582), a friend of St. John of the Cross, was one of the first to distinguish the various degrees of mental prayer and is regarded as giving the most down to earth advice on the mystical way. In her autobiography, *The Book of Her Life,* she draws the analogy between mental prayer and a garden to illustrate the amount of effort we need to put into prayer. The beginner in prayer is like a gardener starting to cultivate barren and weed-filled ground. The Lord, she says, pulls up the weeds and plants good seeds. It is with his help that we must strive to make them grow, taking care to irrigate them with the water he provides.

St. Teresa mentions four ways of watering the garden: from a well, by a water wheel, a stream, or rain. Beginners in prayer are like those who draw water from a well. This requires the hardest work, as we have to become disciplined in prayer, repent of our sins, meditate on the life of Christ, and have an earnest desire to serve God. Like the water wheel, which requires less effort, the second degree of prayer occurs when we submit totally to God's will, receiving his joy and peace. The work is minimal when the garden is fed by a stream, and in this third degree of prayer, the activity on our part is to be completely occupied with God and rejoice at being in his presence. "This prayer," St. Teresa says, "is a glorious foolishness, a heavenly madness where the true wisdom is learned . . ." (16:1). At this level "the prayer is not experienced as work but as glory" (18:1). When rain falls, the gardener is relieved of watering. Similarly, in the final degree of prayer no effort is required on our part. God himself provides the communication by bringing us into union with him. He absorbs our whole being in his majesty to the point where even the expression of joy would be a distraction. St. Teresa describes how through this union she was sometimes carried out of her body, her soul ascending to heaven in a state of spiritual ecstasy, rapture, or flight, during which she even levitated on rare occasions (20:4f).

Many of us are fascinated by supernatural phenomena such as levitation, stigmata (the wounds of the crucified Christ), bilocation (being present in two locations simultaneously), visions, and existing solely on the Communion host, which have been associated with mysticism. But we must be careful not to make them the yardstick of mystical experience.

On one occasion, a young woman described to me the hours she spent in a trance-like state before a picture of the Virgin Mary. The figure, she said, would sometimes talk to her, telling her that if her friends only had faith, they, too, would be able to share in the vision. Her prayer life had become dominated by the picture.

I have also met many young people who have justified their use of hallucinogens as a short-cut to mystical experiences. They claimed that it heightened their spiritual awareness, but it seemed to me that they were more interested in enjoying the highs of a drug-induced trip than in worshiping and serving God. Like the Jews that St. Paul criticized (1 Cor 1:22), they were seeking signs.

Although we need to be open to God's revealing himself in diverse ways, it is a mistake to think that Christian mysticism is a question of special signs and revelations. Most true mystics have been embarrassed by such phenomena, since they feel that they distract from their primary aim: union with God. St. John of the Cross advises that any thoughts, feelings, or supernatural manifestations are an obstacle to overcome:

> Insofar as he is capable, a person must void himself of all, so that however many supernatural communications he receives, he will continually live as though denuded of them and in darkness (*The Ascent of Mount Carmel*, II:4:2).

Levitation is not mentioned in *The Interior Castle*, St. Teresa's final and most highly regarded work. Here she extends the classifications of prayer through the analogy of a castle within us. God dwells at the center, and the many rooms or dwelling places surrounding him represent seven spiritual stages. Entry to the castle is through prayer. The first three dwelling places symbolize what we can do through our own efforts and God's grace. In the first set of rooms are those who are worldly but speak to God from time to time. In the second are those who have begun to practice the art of prayer, while the third suite is occupied by those who persevere in prayer.

The remaining four dwelling places deal with contemplative states of prayer. When we reach the fourth group of rooms we begin to look within ourselves to find God, "where He is found more easily and in a way more beneficial to us than when sought in creatures . . ." (IV:3:3). Brief union with God marks the fifth group of rooms, in which we become detached from ourselves and our surroundings, and are able to rest in God. In the sixth set God gives us the courage to be betrothed to him as a mystical spouse, and leads us into spiritual ecstasy, in which "the soul was never so awake to the things of God nor did it have such deep enlightenment and knowledge of His majesty" (VI:4:4). In the seventh suite, which is God's dwelling place, we are made one with him in mystical marriage.

Many other Christian mystics who are worth reading include the fourteenth century anchoress Juliana of Norwich, the anonymous author of *The Cloud of Unknowing*, Meister Eckhart (1260–1328), St. Bonaventure (1221–1274), St. Jane Frances de Chantal (1572–1641), Brother Lawrence of the Resurrection (1611–1691), and Jean-Pierre de Caussade (1675–1751), and, in this century, Charles de Foucauld, and the stigmatist, Padre Pio. By sampling their writings, you will come to a fuller understanding, not only of mystical prayer, but of prayer generally.

THE JESUS PRAYER

Lord Jesus Christ, Son of God, have mercy on me, a sinner—the Gospel message is said to be embodied in this short, ancient prayer. Because of its brevity, it is easily understood and remembered, and can be said at any time and in any place. The Jesus Prayer can be effective during those dry spells when we find it difficult to pray, and for refocusing on God when our thoughts begin to wander. It is among the most versatile of all prayers, for it can be used as a warm-up, as a close-up meditation, as a one-liner, as centering prayer (see *Contemplation*), or as a background mantra for contemplation.

St. Simeon, the early fifteenth century archbishop of Thessalonica, stresses that these dozen words are among the most significant that we can pray:

> It is a prayer and a vow and a confession of faith, conferring upon us the Holy Spirit and divine gifts, cleansing the heart, driving out devils. It is the indwelling presence of Jesus Christ within us, and a fountain of spiritual reflections and divine thoughts. It is remission of sins, healing of soul and body, and shining of divine illumination; it is a well of God's mercy, bestowing upon the humble revelations and initiation into the mysteries of God. It is our only salvation, for it contains within itself the saving Name of Our God, the only Name upon which we call, the Name of Jesus Christ the Son of God (*The Art of Prayer*, pp. 88–89).

The Jesus Prayer has its origins in the Gospels. Bartimaeus appealed to Jesus, "Jesus, Son of David, have pity on me" (Mk 10:47; Lk 18:39). The lepers offered similar prayers (Lk 17:13), and the tax collector beat his breast and said, "God, be merciful to me, a sinner" (Lk 18:13). Several of the Desert Fathers prayed the name of Jesus, and the phrase *Lord, have mercy* (Kyrie eleison) was used as a congregational response in the Eucharists of the early Church. But the two parts of the Jesus Prayer—the invocation of the various names of Jesus, and the acknowledgement of our need for his loving mercy—did not appear together until the sixth century in the work of Abba Philemon. Sometimes the text is abbreviated to *Lord Jesus Christ, have mercy on me, Jesus Lord Jesus Christ, Jesus . . . Mercy,* or the early Fathers' practice of using just the name of Jesus. It is often prayed in these shortened forms as a centering word or phrase.

Let us now take a close look at the words of the prayer:

Lord: Here we are acknowledging, like doubting Thomas when he met the risen Christ, that Jesus is our Lord and that God is the master and ruler of our lives.

Jesus: The name Jesus literally means "God saves" and underlines Christ's saving mission. But as it was also a relatively common Jewish name, it reminds us of how God took ordinary human form and came to dwell among us.

Christ: This is a special title reserved for anointed kings of Israel. The Jews of Jesus' time were awaiting a savior-king or messiah to overcome Roman rule. Jesus, however, had a different type of salvation in mind. As he told Pilate, "Mine is not a kingdom of this world" (Jn 18:36). The kingdom that Christ sought was over our hearts, minds, and souls.

Son of God: This title reinforces Jesus' unique relationship with God: "The Father and I

Have mercy: are one" (Jn 10:30). It is through Jesus that we receive God's forgiveness and redemption.

Have mercy: By asking for mercy, we are admitting our dependence on God. His mercy includes love, compassion, kindness, and attentiveness to our needs, as well as forgiveness.

On me: This is your private request to God, as each of us needs to ask for and accept his loving mercy. Sometimes the plural *us* is substituted to bring home that we have all sinned and fallen short of the glory of God (Rom 3:23).

A sinner: We need to approach God in humility, taking a realistic view of ourselves and the ways in which we have offended him.

One objection that has been raised against the Jesus Prayer is that it dwells on our sinfulness rather than the positive aspects of our faith, like joy and hope. Yet, the writer of St. John's Epistle reminds us, "If we say we have no sin in us, we are deceiving ourselves and refusing to admit the truth" (1 Jn 1:8). That means that each of us has to recognize that it is only through Christ's sacrifice that we receive God's mercy. Our joy and hope come from knowing that we are forgiven and loved.

Although the Jesus Prayer is not normally used as a close-up meditation, you might begin this way to gain an intellectual grasp of its implications before using it in the more traditional manner. In Eastern Orthodox practice, the prayer is repeated over and over as a *mantra* or *mantram,* a sacred formula recited inaudibly. To those unfamiliar with the prayer, this may seem like unnecessary parroting, an insult to our intelligence and to God, but the constant reiteration serves as a vehicle to draw us into God's presence. Used in this way, the Jesus Prayer is a form of contemplation. It is therefore important to seek the guidance of an experienced spiritual director if you propose to say the prayer for extended periods.

The fourteenth century monks on Mount Athos, or the hesychasts as they are often called, suggested that the prayer be said with the head lowered and the gaze directed toward the heart, while synchronizing the words of the prayer to the breathing and the heartbeat. The unknown nineteenth century Russian peasant who wrote *The Way of a Pilgrim,* one of the best practical guides on the Jesus Prayer, gives us this clear outline of the procedure, which you might like to try:

> ... imagine your heart; direct your eyes as though you were looking at it through your breast, see the heart as vividly as you can, and listen attentively to its rhythmic beat. And when you have become accustomed to this, then begin to say the words of the Prayer, while looking into your heart, to the rhythm of your heartbeat. With the first beat say "Lord," with the second "Jesus," with the third "Christ," with the fourth "have mercy," and with the fifth "on me." And repeat this frequently....
> The next step, according to the writings of the Fathers, is to direct the flow of the Jesus Prayer in the heart in harmony with your breathing; that is, while inhaling say, "Lord Jesus Christ," and while exhaling say, "have mercy on me." Practice this as often as possible, gradually increasing the time, and before too long you will experience a kind of pleasant pain in the heart, a warmth, and a sense of burning. Thus, with the help of God, you will attain self-activating prayer of the heart. However, you must be extremely careful in all this to guard your imagination against any kind of visions; the holy Fathers strictly warn against this so as not to fall into deception (p. 83).

The importance of avoiding mental images is frequently mentioned by Orthodox writers. Yet this is easier said than done. When I first heard of the Jesus Prayer, I was very dubious about its effectiveness. It seemed to have overtones of a magical incantation. I was finally encouraged to experiment with it (if that's the right word) during a weekend retreat at a monastery. As I began *Lord Jesus Christ, Son of God, have mercy on me, a sinner; Lord Jesus Christ, Son of God . . .* , I felt like a record stuck in a groove.

To try to give the whole exercise some relevance, I would pick out a word from the prayer and connect it with scenes from the Gospels. "Christ" brought to mind Jesus' interrogation before the Sanhedrin when he was asked, "Are you the Christ?" "A sinner" got me thinking about Mary Magdalene and others Jesus had forgiven, as well as my own shortcomings.

Every so often I would remember my instruction on how the prayer was to be said and analyze what was happening. Then I would wonder if I should be doing this kind of analysis. The advice of Bishop Theophan the Recluse (1815–1894) kept resurfacing. He had related his own difficulties in dispelling images and found that the way to rise above this was to be conscious of God within. "This awareness of the eye of God looking down on your inner being," he had said, "must not be accompanied by any visual concept, but must be confined to a simple conviction or feeling" (*The Art of Prayer*, p. 100). Eventually I found the images fading into the background and felt myself in the divine presence. There were no flashing lights or overwhelming feelings of jubilation—only a quiet, peaceful realization of being surrounded by Christ. Even after I left the chapel, for days afterward I still found myself repeating the prayer, like a pop song that kept playing in my head. The Jesus Prayer continued to fill me with an awareness of the love of Christ.

HEALING

A major crisis will push most of us to the brink of prayer. We can quite literally be brought to our knees. This is especially true when we or someone we love is facing a tragedy or lies gravely ill. A grandmother dying of cancer, a bereaved widow, a prematurely born infant, or a youth who is about to have wisdom teeth extracted—these are typical of the kinds of cries for help that appear on Church prayer lists and in our prayers.

Jesus promised that prayer will be answered. "If you have faith, everything you ask for in prayer you will receive" (Mt 21:22). But although God will always respond to our prayers, we need to be careful not to expect instant miracles. Prayer is not a quick fix elixir, as if all we had to do is utter a few prayerful formulas, have a bit of faith, and "presto!"—maybe another miracle from God! We can make our requests to him, but it is God who decides. As much as we might like prayer to be an "open sesame" to health and good fortune, God could have other plans.

The Jews of Jesus' time believed that illness and misfortune were God's punishment for sin. But Jesus was able to show that the hurtful effects of sin could be overcome. The miraculous healings described in the New Testament—casting out demons, restoring sight, hearing, and the ability to walk—demonstrated that through Jesus the power of sin can be broken. This can be seen in the story of the paralytic who was lowered through the roof of the building where Jesus was preaching (Mk 2:1-12). Jesus' first words to the afflicted man were: "My child, your sins are forgiven." Some of the Jewish leaders regarded this as blasphemous, and they reproached him, asking: "Who can forgive sins but

God?" Jesus replied with another question, "Which of these is easier: to say to the paralytic 'Your sins are forgiven' or to say 'Get up, pick up your stretcher and walk'?" He was making the point that forgiveness of sins is a prerequisite to healing.

The curing of the paralytic is a parable for us all. We need to have faith that God will forgive, and that we can be reconciled with him no matter what we have done. Although most of us no longer accept that God punishes us deliberately by inflicting illness or tragedy—these happen by accident, self-neglect, human violence, or a quirk of nature—we should still make reconciliation with God our first priority.

If we have an infirmity or some other complaint, instead of launching straight into prayer for healing and handing God a list of broken legs, tumors, heart disorders or emotional problems, and then sitting back to see what kind of answer God will come up with, we should begin by committing ourselves to him. Because so many of us need to be assured of his love and forgiveness, you might prefer to make your confession before a priest and receive his counsel. Approach God like a child, in total trust and faith, ask for his forgiveness, and *accept* it. By doing this, you are healing your relationship with God and removing the barriers created by your sin. You have now changed the emphasis from what God can do for you to what you can do for God. It is only then that you should consider mentioning your specific petitions, as now you will be open to receive the answer. You are putting yourself at God's disposal and trusting in him implicitly, rather than pinning your hopes on an instant miracle. Whether or not you or your loved ones are cured is no longer the primary issue.

I remember an English family who made a special pilgrimage to the shrine of Lourdes with their mentally retarded and spastic daughter, Becky. When they returned home, there was no visible improvement in Becky's condition. The change was in the parents. "What we have gained as a family," her mother told me, "is far more important than having Becky walking and talking like other children. Of course it would be lovely if that would happen, but going to Lourdes renewed our faith. We gave ourselves to God, just accepting his love instead of expecting a miracle. The wonder of his love comes over you: *that* is the great miracle." A healing did take place—to Becky's parents.

The extraordinary will sometimes occur. A cancerous growth can shrivel, a terminally ill patient might be restored to health, the bereaved can receive God's consolation, or arthritics may move their joints without pain. Many who are ill and troubled find that once they have surrendered to God's love, they are no longer occupied with their problems and worried about what the future will hold. Their trust in God brings about an inner peace. This reduction of anxiety will often contribute to a cure, since numerous disorders are anxiety related, among them colitis, ulcers, migraines, hypertension, asthma, skin conditions, insomnia, and especially neurosis. You will also find that if you are a heavy smoker or drinker, a compulsive overeater, or have some other form of addiction, your attitude toward yourself will change once you have turned your life over to God. You will see how your body is, in St. Paul's words, a "temple" in need of proper care (2 Cor 6:16).

Much of the pain and suffering in our lives comes from broken relationships—death, divorce, shattered romances, splintered families. The death of a loved one is especially hard to bear. It leaves us feeling empty and alone. Our anguish seems insurmountable. In such distressing circumstances, it can be difficult to trust in God's love. Yet this is a time when you shouldn't hide your feelings from him. Pour out all your anger, remorse, resentment, and guilt, and ask for his help. Remember that you will not be the only one who is affected; include in your prayers the others who are also suffering. It can take time to accept God's healing love, but try to remain open to this. You could give thanks for the life of the person who has died and offer to God your memories. You might also want to include in your prayers those who have comforted you during your bereavement.

In another kind of broken relationship, a friend of mine and his sister had a falling out. It began with a discussion about family finances, but when neither side was prepared to compromise, it degenerated into snide comments and angry reactions. When a situation like this occurs, it is essential to detach yourself from your own point of view and see it from the other person's perspective. Even if you feel that your position is valid, don't attempt to justify it in your own mind. Instead, ask for God's guidance in helping to understand what happened. When you have calmed down, review the conflict and try to see how the things you did or said could have hurt the other person. Perhaps my friend had unwittingly implied that he was superior to his sister since he held a good job while she was unemployed, or that she was unwilling to take on her share of the family responsibilities. Often it is not what we say that causes the problem, but how it is understood. Try to imagine how you would feel if the roles were reversed—if you had spent the last month sending out resumés and knocking on doors of dozens of firms desperately looking for work, and had to swallow your pride and accept a subsidy from your parents. You might not be able to put yourself entirely in the other person's shoes, but unless you realize how you might be insensitive, reconciliation is going to be difficult. Then ask for God's forgiveness and guidance in effecting a reconciliation. When you have done this, you will be in a better position to ask the other person for forgiveness or accept an apology. Treat your conflict as a positive experience from which you can learn how to be more understanding in the future.

In the case of my friend, his sister was so hurt that a year later she still was not communicating with him and at first refused to attend his wedding. It might take time to build up trust in each other again. If your efforts fail, don't poison yourself with blame or bear a grudge. Offer the problem to God and leave it with him. Jesus tells us, "Come to me, all you who labor and are overburdened, and I will give you rest" (Mt 11:28), so why not take his advice?

In the Epistle of James we are told that if anyone is ill, he should "send for the elders of the Church, and they must anoint him with oil in the name of the Lord and pray over him" (Jas 5:14). Many denominations practice the sacrament of anointing, private communion and confession, the laying on of hands, or other types of healing services. If you are in need of any type of healing, you could explore these possibilities. Some faith healers profess to be endowed with curative powers. Check their claims and motives

Laying on of Hands

carefully. Is their emphasis on soliciting contributions or putting
the spotlight on themselves? Or is it on spreading God's love and
salvation as part of a recognized church? But in the case of demonic possession, you will need to seek professional assistance
from a psychologist, psychiatrist, or pastor. Most clergy are psy-
chologically sensitive and will know when an expert exorcist
should be called in. Fortunately, these occasions are rare.

If you are praying for healing for other people, try to pray together, as this will help reassure them of God's love and that they are
part of his caring family. If this is not possible, visualize the people while you pray. Be ready for the Holy Spirit to lead you into
some practical course of action, like helping with chores during a
family time of need, bringing flowers, or offering companionship

and support. In these ways you will be participating in the healing process.

Whatever the outcome of your petitions to God, don't forget to give thanks. When Jesus cured the ten lepers (Lk 17:11–19), only one returned to thank him. Don't be like the other nine.

MAKING DECISIONS

The choice of a career, which college to attend, whether to get married, whom to marry, and where to live—these are the kinds of major decisions many of us have trouble making. Sometimes a simple question to God can uncover the right decision (see *One-Liners*). If, however, the problem seems complex and you can see no simple answer, the following procedure may be helpful.

First, ask God for his guidance in making your choice. Then find out as much as you can about each of the alternatives that you are considering. If, for example, you are trying to make up your mind whether to go into journalism or the computer field, check on what is involved in each type of work (such as hours, salary, contact with people, and scope for challenge and growth), whether you have the talents or could acquire the skills and qualifications which are necessary, whether your personality is suited for the work, what the opportunities are and how long it takes to train, and how much competition there is in the job market.

When you have set out the factors for and against each choice, evaluate them in terms of how well they fit in with your goals in life. Be realistic. Is your emphasis on bringing home a bigger paycheck, working in a congenial environment, spending more time with your family and friends, serving the community, or being an effective witness to God's love? At times it may seem like comparing oranges and bicycles—but try to list your priorities in order. This will help you to have a more detached, objective view of the possibilities.

One of the biggest difficulties that we face in making decisions is in trying to gauge how we really feel about the alternatives. Suppose that you are deciding whether or not to become engaged. You might have listed powerful positive reasons for making the commitment, such as strong mutual physical attraction, enjoyment of one another's company, some common interests, and the approval of family and friends. On the debit side, you might have noted financial irresponsibility, heavy smoking, and lukewarm Christian faith. How can you resolve this dilemma? To help clarify your emotions, imagine that you have made your decision and that you are now married. Think of all that this really involves. Would you enjoy spending most of your free time together, pooling financial resources and decisions, and sharing the chores? How would you feel about the disruptions to your life style of having constantly to consider the other person and the home life which you are jointly building? Would you find fulfillment in bringing up your children together? Can you imagine your love growing through the good times and the bad, in sickness and in health, until you are parted by death? Continue to explore your reactions to this imagined situation for several days. Then try living with the opposite choice. Would you be very upset if you went your separate ways? Would you feel that a light had gone out of your life, and that you might never again meet anyone with whom you were so compatible? Or would you feel a little relieved at avoiding making such an important commitment at this stage, and pleased to have the opportunity to spend more time with other people and on different activities instead?

Now bring your problem and your priorities to God in prayer again. It could help at this stage to refer to the Bible or to seek the counsel of other Christians. If possible, allow a few days of breathing space to elapse and then re-examine your priorities.

You might want to make a few changes. At this stage a pattern should begin to emerge.

Be prepared to end up with a totally different course of action from any of the options you might have outlined. A teacher in my parish who had been trying to make up her mind between several educational positions in terms of salary and work benefits had nearly reached a decision when she began to have second thoughts. She asked for God's guidance, and several days later she had her answer. It came while she was casually flicking through a Church magazine. An article on the need for missionary teachers caught her eye, and she soon found herself teaching for the Church in a third world country for a fraction of the salary she would have earned in the United States. When we allow God to guide us in our decisions, we open ourselves to unexpected possibilities.

SECTION V

Charismatic Prayer

PRAYING IN TONGUES

"I was so filled with the Holy Spirit that the words just flowed."
This was how one man described his experience of praying in
tongues. The words he spoke sounded like an exotic language,
which few, if any, would understand: *By yung bah stay les kros-
tanday shong doh foh. Bing dy kray.*

Praying in tongues or glossolalia is mentioned several times in the
New Testament (Acts 2:4; 10:46; 19:6; 1 Cor 12 and 14). But even
though St. Paul listed tongues and the ability to interpret them
among the nine gifts of the Holy Spirit, by the third century the
practice had fallen into disuse. It wasn't until the beginning of
this century that praying in tongues re-emerged, to gain widespread popularity within the last few decades through the charismatic and pentecostal movements.

The key attraction of glossolalia is the assurance it brings that the
Holy Spirit is working through us. "I used to think that prayer
was speaking politely with God," a middle-aged charismatic told
me. "The relationship was dry and distant. It was only after I surrendered to the Spirit and received the gift of tongues that I realized I had been making it difficult for myself. I was so busy
thinking about what to say to God that I wasn't allowing the Spirit to speak through me. Now I know he's within me."

Learning to pray in tongues is not a question of inventing an ob-
scure, secret code in order to communicate with God. Neither is
it imitating the prayerful utterances of those who already have
the gift of tongues. The words must come from the Holy Spirit. So

you will need to open yourself to the Spirit in total trust and be prepared to accept how he will lead you.

You could begin by praying out loud in your own language. This helps to overcome self-consciousness about praying in tongues. Ask God to grant you this gift, and then remain silent, refraining from using any language you have learned. After a time you will probably find that you want to express your feelings to God. Don't just sit back waiting for something to happen, but open your mouth and speak out in the confidence that the Lord will give you the words. Many beginners launch into inarticulate babble, by fluttering the tongue or pronouncing the same syllables over and over. To get beyond this preliminary phase, Fr. John H. Hampsch, a prominent charismatic preacher, recommends eliminating repetitions and letting new syllables flow.

At first you will probably feel that you are making the words up, and will want to deny that it is a gift from God, but continue to trust that through the power of the Holy Spirit he is giving you the words to praise and adore him.

St. Paul offers some cautionary advice about using tongues in the Christian community. "I thank God," he says, "that I have a greater gift of tongues than all of you, but when I am in the presence of the community I would rather say five words that mean something than ten thousand words in a tongue" (1 Cor 14:18–19). Paul warns that the utterances are usually unintelligible to others, and non-believers might think that the speaker is mad. For this reason, he says, those who pray in tongues at church meetings should also pray for the power of interpretation (1 Cor 14:24f). Usually the gift of interpreting a prophecy in tongues will come from another Christian, so if you feel that the Holy Spirit is speaking through you to the community, take heed of Paul's advice and listen to those known for their gifts of wisdom, interpretation, and discernment. Remember that the Spirit works through others as well as you.

In rare instances it is claimed that tongue-speakers have communicated in a recognizable foreign language which they have never been taught. While this might happen, linguistic studies by

William J. Samarin have not substantiated these claims. He concluded that glossolalia consists of "strings of syllables made up of sounds taken from among all those that the speaker knows, put together more or less haphazardly" (*Tongues of Men and Angels: The Religious Language of Pentecostalism*, p. 227).

After the first few months, you might find that you are praying in tongues less and less. If this happens, don't try to force the tongues. The Spirit may be leading you into a period of quiet communion where you can rest in the Lord (see *Contemplation*), or to communicate in some other way.

SECTION VI

Asian Prayer Techniques

TRANSCENDENTAL MEDITATION

Many Christians are suspicious of the methods of other religions. They feel that if they borrow the method, they must also accept the doctrine. This simply isn't true. Don't forget that Christianity throughout history has absorbed customs and ideas of other religions and philosophies, and has taken the best from them to use to the glory of God.

Transcendental Meditation, an updated version of the basic teaching of Sankara's eighth century Advait school of Vedantic thought, was popularized in the West by the Maharishi Mahesh Yogi. When he first introduced it as the Spiritual Regeneration Movement in the United States in 1958, it barely got off the ground because of its close ties with Hinduism. He dropped most of the religious elements and reintroduced it in 1962 as Transcendental Meditation—a simple, quickly mastered technique "for gaining a state of deep rest coupled with heightened alertness" (*Happiness: The TM Program, Psychiatry and Enlightment,* p. 98). Since then, it has grown in popularity, and well over a million people worldwide have been trained in the method.

Proponents of TM enthusiastically describe how it has changed their lives. "It brightens your life generally, helps you to relax, increase your attention span, communicate and be more sensitive to yourself and others," one instructor explained to me. The Maharishi contends that his method is a practical, natural, and scientifically validated formula for living in a suffering and troubled world. He supports this claim by pointing to studies of drug addicts, alcoholics, and criminals whose lives have been transformed by TM. If one percent of the population were to practice

117

TM for a few minutes morning and evening and live in an orderly and intelligent way for the rest of the day, the Maharishi asserts, then the Age of Enlightment—good health, abundant love and happiness, the elimination of war, crime, and all negative behavior—would follow. Other claims include improved academic performance, increased productivity, faster reactions and more acute perceptual ability, better psychological health, lowered blood pressure in hypertensive patients, and decreased anxiety.

Although there are many books about the benefits of TM, the details of the method are closely guarded, and training is available only through recognized TM Centers. These are listed in the phone directory. Be prepared to pay a fee (which isn't exactly cheap) for your instruction. Here is what will take place.

Before you can enroll in a course, you must attend two free introductory lectures, in which the virtues of TM are extolled. If you go ahead and register in the course, you will go through an initiation rite with Hindu overtones, for which you will be asked to bring flowers, fruit, and a white handkerchief. At this time you will be interviewed and assigned a mantra, a Sanskrit word whose meaning will not be revealed to you. You are expected to keep your mantra confidential. Nevertheless, it is likely to be a short word with soft consonants such as *rama, sham, aing, hirèem,* or possibly the famous Buddhist and Yoga mantra, *om.* Since the mantras are meaningless to most Westerners, they will conjure up no imagery and do not distract. The mantra should keep your mind on one track and minimize competing thoughts. Its constant repetition sets up a rhythm, so that you can feel at peace with yourself and detached from your surroundings.

You should be prepared to commit yourself to twenty minutes of meditation twice a day. The procedure is simple. Sit comfortably, eyes closed, for a minute to allow yourself to quiet down. Then silently repeat your mantra at whatever speed suits you. You might try coordinating the mantra with your breathing. Don't be concerned if your thoughts wander. Just return to your mantra as soon as you realize what is happening. To come out of your meditation, stop saying the mantra and remain still for several minutes while you gradually attune yourself to your surroundings. Then open your eyes. You should now feel as if awakening from a refreshing sleep.

After a few scheduled group meetings, you will gain practice and confidence in the technique. If necessary, you can return to the Center for brush-up sessions. There are also classes for children, as well as advanced adult programs, some lasting several months, for those who wish to refine their technique and pursue the Maharishi's philosophy of Cosmic Consciousness.

TM is not a prayer method. Some Christians, however, have found that it has given them serenity and a heightened inclination to pray. In this sense, it can function as a warm-up. But think carefully before investing in a TM program. The benefits claimed are probably similar to those of many Christian prayer techniques, especially contemplation and the Jesus Prayer. The significant difference is that Christian spirituality is concerned with fostering communion with God, whereas TM is aimed at attaining self-contentment.

Can TM be adapted as a prayer technique? According to the TM organization, the answer is a resounding no; if there is any modification, it is no longer TM. Many Christians, on the other hand, have successfully substituted a meaningful Christian word in place of the Sanskrit mantra. The Benedictine John Main has proposed using words in Aramaic, the language of Jesus, like "abba" (literally "papa" or Father) and "maranatha" ("Come, Lord Jesus"). Robert Schuller, pastor of the Garden Grove Community Church (the Crystal Cathedral) in Southern California, suggests "I am, I am" (Ex 3:14). Choose your mantra carefully. Once you have made your choice, stick with it, for as St. Gregory of Sinai (c. 1290–1346) cautions, "Trees that are frequently transplanted don't grow roots." Experienced meditators advise that over a period of time, with constant repetition, the mantra becomes so ingrained that you are no longer just saying the word. You *become* your mantra.

YOGA

There is more to yoga than standing on your head or tying your-self up in knots. "I admit, I first became involved in yoga as a challenge," one religion teacher told me. "I've always been agile, and frankly I wanted to see if I could manage some of those out-landish positions. It was only later that I began to appreciate it as an aid to my prayers."

In Sanskrit, yoga means "yoke," the uniting of body, mind, and soul to the Divine Spirit. It is a means of controlling the mind and senses so that we can be in harmony with ourselves and God. The ancient Hindu scriptures, the *Upanishads*, describe it this way:

> When all senses are stilled, when the mind is at rest, when the intellect wavers not—then, say the wise, is reached the highest state. This calm of the senses and the mind has been defined as yoga. He who attains it is freed from delusion (*Kathopanishad*).

But although yoga is mentioned in these pre-fifth century B.C. scriptures, it was not until the second century B.C. that yoga was developed into a systematic method by Patanjali. In the 1880's yoga was introduced into the United States by Swami Viveken-anda, who founded the Vedanta Society, a Hindu movement that attracted many literary figures in the 1950's, such as Aldous Hux-ley. The religious elements, however, have generally taken a back seat in the Western world, where yoga has been promoted as a means to health and serenity, rather than union with God. Nevertheless, some Christians have adopted yoga techniques when they pray, replacing the Hindu concept of the Universal Spirit with the Holy Trinity.

There are various forms of yoga—karma yoga, the way of action; jnana yoga, the way of knowledge; bhakti yoga, the way of devotion and faith; japa yoga, which emphasizes mantric chanting; laya or kundalini yoga, which concentrates on hidden power centers within the body; raja yoga, literally "the king of yoga," which combines many elements of the other schools in an eight point program toward perfection. These eight points or "limbs" include observing moral commandments, self-discipline and purification, postures, controlled breathing, detachment, concentration on a fixed point, meditation or contemplation, and *samadhi* or superconscious union with the subject of contemplation. Fr. Herbert Slade of the Anglican Cowley Fathers in Oxford describes in *Exploration into Contemplative Prayer* how his order has adapted these eight limbs into Christian contemplative life. The program is too involved to summarize here, but if you are interested in adopting a yogic style of prayer, it is worth examining.

The form of yoga that has become popular in the West is the simplest and most basic, hatha yoga, which emphasizes the breathing exercises or *pranayamas*, and eighty-four stylized postures or *asanas*. Here is a fundamental hatha yoga breathing exercise. You might like to try it to help you relax, be more alert, and able to concentrate during prayer. Lie on your back on the floor and exhale, pulling in your abdomen as tightly as you can to expel the air through your mouth and nose. When you feel that there is no more air left, imagine that you have a birthday cake with candles ablaze, and try to blow them all out. Then, as though there were one more candle, blow again without taking another breath. Your lungs should now be empty. Then close your mouth, and begin breathing through your nose, trying to fill the lungs completely. Now breathe out through your nostrils, and repeat the process until you feel a little lightheaded. (This is because of the oversupply of oxygen to the brain.) Relax for a while; then try the procedure several more times.

Next, you might try some of the postures. It is preferable to receive training from a competent teacher or *guru*, one who can lead you from darkness (gu) toward enlightenment (ru = light). You might also learn the basics from one of the many self-instruction manuals (see *Further Reading*). Don't feel compelled to master all the postures. For Christians, the most valuable will be the lotus position or one of its variations. Because the spine is kept in perfect alignment and the circulation remains unimpeded, these sitting positions provide the best way of keeping the body still for prolonged periods of prayer. For this reason they are ideal for extended meditation and contemplation. As the lotus is a unique position it can serve to put you in a prayerful mood, in the same way that a chapel might.

The half-lotus is the best way to begin:

    1. Sit on the floor with your legs outstretched. You might prefer to sit on a small cushion or even a tele-

Half-Lotus

phone book to help you get into position and avoid resting on your heels.

2. Grasp your left foot in your hands and place your left heel against the perineum (the area between the genitals and the anus), with the sole against the inside of your right thigh.

3. Now bend the right leg and cross it over the left ankle, keeping the right heel against the abdomen.

4. Position the sole of your right foot in the cleft between the thigh and calf of your left leg.

5. Rest your hands on your knees.

At first you will be lucky if you can get your legs in place and keep your knees on the floor. You will need to ease yourself into the position over a period of weeks, as your muscles loosen up. Your knees will almost certainly hurt on your first attempts, but don't force yourself if it is too painful. Some stretching exercises for the legs might be helpful. Once you have mastered the half-lotus, you could graduate to the full lotus.

1. Sit on the floor with the legs extended, as in the half-lotus.

2. Grasp the right foot and place it at the base of the thigh so that your right heel is near your navel.

3. Grasp your left foot and bring it over the right leg to the base of your right thigh, the heel being near the navel.

4. The soles of both feet should be turned upward.

5. To extricate yourself from this posture, reverse the procedure.

It is advisable to alternate the legs from time to time, so that they are evenly exercised.

If you wish to go beyond the physical aspects of hatha yoga, you might like to try some of the concentration, meditation, and con-

Full Lotus

templative techniques of raja yoga. A favorite discipline for
strengthening the ability to concentrate is the candle exercise.
Place a lighted candle about three feet in front of you. Gaze directly at the flame for about two minutes. Then close your eyes
and cover them with the palms of your hands. For the next two
minutes retain the mental image of the flame. Try not to let the
image disappear, but if this happens, without looking at the candle again, try to recall it in your imagination. Repeat this each
time your mind begins to wander. With practice you will be able
to minimize or eliminate distractions altogether—a skill that can
be readily transferred to your prayer life. You could also substitute other objects for the candle.

Yoga meditations are usually divided into those with "seed," in
which we are actively focusing on a thought, image, or object, or
"seedless," in which the mind is emptied of all ideas and images,
and is filled with a simple awareness of God. One meditation with
seed is the multi-petaled lotus flower. Here is a Christian form of
it. When you are completely relaxed, select a word which has a

Christian connotation, such as cross, bread, wine, water, blood, tomb, or mercy. Make this word the center of your lotus, and let an association come freely to mind. If you choose wine for the lotus center, you might make the connection with grapes. This association would be the first petal of the lotus. Don't dwell longer than five seconds on any association; this is not meant to be an in-depth analysis. Now return to the center again, avoiding any linking of thoughts with the petal words, and make another association. This time wine might suggest the blood of Christ. Next time it might be corkscrew, pizza, or the wedding feast at Cana. You can't foresee which direction these associations will take. Always go back to the center before adding another petal word. Continue this exercise for no more than a quarter of an hour. When you are finished you will probably be surprised at the mental connections you have made. You might gain some interesting insights into yourself and your faith.

Lotus Flower

A seedless meditation is a form of contemplation. In Hindu practice, this involves rising above all conscious thoughts and images to reach a state of harmony with ourselves and creation. "There remains no sense of 'I' or 'mine,' as the working of the body, the mind, and the intellect have stopped as if one is in deep sleep," explains B.K.S. Iyengar, one of the best known yoga teachers. He adds that "there is only the experience of consciousness, truth, and unutterable joy. There is a peace that passeth all understanding. . . . Yoga has departed from the material world and has merged with the eternal. There is then no duality between the knower and the known, for they are merged like camphor and the flame" (*Light on Yoga,* p. 54).

If you wish to use yoga techniques for contemplation, you will need to bear in mind that as a Christian your aim is surrendering to God's love and his will, rather than passively accepting your place in creation.

ZEN

"What is the sound of one hand clapping?" This is the kind of riddle a Zen master might give a pupil to lead him or her toward enlightenment or *satori*—the aim of Zen.

Zen is a sect of Mahayana Buddhism, the Northern school, which according to legend was brought to China in the sixth century by the Indian philosopher Bodhidarma, from which it spread to Japan by the twelfth century. It was introduced into the United States at the World Parliament of Religions at the Chicago Exposition in 1893, but did not gain widespread popularity in America until several decades later.

Enlightenment is not attained through rational thought, but through an intuitive experience of ourselves and the world about us. One of the best known authorities on Zen, Daisetz Suzuki, says that "with satori our entire surroundings are viewed from quite an unexpected angle of perception. Whatever this is, the world for those who have gained a satori is no more the old world as it used to be" (*Zen Buddhism*, p. 84). In a very minor way, we can experience satori when, after wrestling with a problem for many days, the solution comes all at once—the light suddenly dawns and we have a "Eureka!" experience.

This new insight is unlikely to be an emotional or cataclysmic affair like St. Paul's conversion on the road to Damascus. A Zen student might experience many satoris, gaining a new revelation each time. The Zen master or *roshi* guides the student toward enlightenment. Through a series of questions, he makes certain that their satoris are real and not imitations, and that the students do not become stuck in any experience. As Buddhists do not believe in a deity, the satori would not be in the nature of an insight into the divine.

There are two paths to satori: *zazen* or the sitting discipline of meditation, and the *koans,* the paradoxical riddles. These activities are often done together. Zazen helps to still the restless mind, which has been likened to a chattering monkey, so that we can go beyond our self-image to come to terms with our true nature.

Here is a basic zazen exercise on the breath. Sit in a comfortable position—the lotus, half-lotus, or even in a straight backed chair—and make sure that your head, back, and neck are in a straight line. Spend a few minutes becoming aware of your bodily sensations. Now focus all your attention on your breathing so that you become aware of the air coming in and out of your nostrils. Do not try to change the pattern of your breathing. After a few moments, begin to count each breath silently, counting "one" on the inhalation and "and" on the exhalation, then "two" on the next inhalation and "and" on the exhalation, and so on, up to ten. The counting is merely an aid to focusing on the breath, so if you lose your place, just return to "one" again. Continue this exercise for fifteen to twenty minutes.

In the Book of Genesis, we learn that God blew life into man. It was the presence of his breath, or the spirit of God, which kept mankind alive. When God took breath away, death followed. Anthony De Mello, a Jesuit from India, suggests that when we do the Zen breathing exercise, we should become conscious of drawing in God with every breath. "I want you to reflect now that this air that you are breathing in is charged with the power and the presence of God. . . . Think of the air as of an immense ocean that surrounds you . . . an ocean heavily colored with God's presence and God's being. . . . While you draw the air into your lungs you are drawing God in." Fr. De Mello also offers this interesting variation: "While you breathe out, imagine you are breathing out all your impurities ... your fears ... your negative feelings" (*Sad-hana: A Way to God,* p. 32).

The other main route to satori, the koans, which are said to num-ber seventeen hundred, are normally assigned by a roshi. These seemingly nonsensical riddles—Does the dog have Buddha na-ture? What was your original face before your parents conceived you? If all things can be reduced to one, to what can one be re-duced?—are merely a means of opening the door to satori. Zen masters compare the koan to a brick "with which to knock at a door; when the door is opened, the brick may be thrown away" (*The Spirit of Zen,* p. 64). Usually the student will begin to ap-proach the koan in an intellectual way, looking for symbolic meanings and associations, to try to arrive at a logical solution. A breakthrough can come only when the thinking process has been put aside.

Christians who are familiar with Zen koans have found that their experiences have given them insights into the baffling paradoxes of the Bible. Fr. J.K. Kadowaki has treated these sayings of Jesus in a similar way to koans:

- "It is easier for a camel to pass through the eye of a needle than for a rich man to enter the kingdom of God" (Mk 10:25).
- "Unless a wheat grain falls on the ground and dies, it re-mains only a single grain; but if it dies, it yields a rich har-vest" (Jn 12:24).

William Johnston, author of *Christian Zen,* considers the follow-ing as Christian koans:

- "Follow me, and leave the dead to bury their dead" (Mt 8:22).
- "For anyone who wants to save his life will lose it; but any-one who loses his life for my sake, and for the sake of the Gospel, will save it" (Mk 8:35).
- "This is my body" (Mt 26:26; Mk 14:22; Lk 22:19; 1 Cor 11:24).

Although the Zen koans must be handled at an intuitive level, most of the Christian paradoxes which are thought to resemble koans are in fact only apparent contradictions and can usually be understood rationally. Nevertheless, the methods of Zen can help us attain inner stillness and to go beyond reason to give intuitive insights of what the Gospel message can mean to us personally.

SECTION VII

Praying With Others

TEACHING CHILDREN TO PRAY

"Gentle Jesus, meek and mild, look upon this little child . . ." and "Now I lay me down to sleep . . ." are prayers which many of us repeated as children before being tucked into bed. Our parents taught us to pray, as they themselves had been taught, by handing down these well-known children's prayers. They became our special prayers, and their nightly repetition helped to instill in us the importance of regular prayer.

Most children enjoy memorizing prayers, and teaching these by rote is one way in which we can assist youngsters to begin their prayer life—especially prayers like the Our Father which are needed for participating in community worship. It is vital, however, that we go beyond implanting a set of familiar words to helping young Christians come to understand what these prayers really mean. We should also encourage children to pray in other ways so that they can be flexible in their approach to God and be able to grow in their relationship with him.

If we are to aid children to grow in their prayer life, it is essential to take into account their emotional and intellectual levels. Pre-schoolers are very dependent on their parents and are still learning to cope with the immediate world around them, while the pre-adolescent is starting to think abstractly and to become more independent. So don't make the mistake of trying to force abstract concepts like predestination, salvation, or the Holy Trinity on first graders and then expect them to comprehend those concepts as you do.

When I first learned the Lord's Prayer as a child, I could never understand why so much fuss was made about forgiving people their trespasses, since nobody trespassed on our property, and it seemed such a trivial crime. It was several years before I came to understand what the word "trespass" meant in the context of the prayer. We should also think about the theological implications of any prayers that we teach. Children can become confused if they learn "Gentle Jesus, meek and mild," and later find in the Gospels that this same Jesus took a whip to the money changers in the temple and had harsh words for the Pharisees.

Help your children, or younger brothers and sisters, or godchildren, to create simple, concrete prayers of their own which are related to *their* experiences. Try to spend time with each child reviewing the day and discussing how the events can be incorporated in their prayers. What would they like to thank God for? Did they appreciate their meals, clean clothes, a chance to learn, or an outing to the park? What are some of the things they could mention to God that they are sorry about? Were they selfish or lazy? Did they lose their tempers, upset somebody, or skip their prayers? What special requests do they want to make to God? Do they wish to include other members of the family, a sick friend, or other children who are not as fortunate as they are? Help children understand that whatever is going on in their lives can be included in their prayers.

At an early stage encourage children to pray out loud with you. As the young often become restless and have a limited attention span, schedule short prayer periods or consider praying while walking together. Perhaps the children might want to offer a drawing, or some other creative activity, to God as part of their prayers. It might also help to have visual material available—photographs of the family and the children's friends, flowers from the garden, or even the family pet—as subjects for prayers of thanksgiving and intercession. A good example would be the mealtime grace when you could provide an opportunity for the youngsters to take turns in giving thanks in their own words for the food before them.

Sometimes children will digress during their prayers. Once when I was listening to my niece pray, she began "Gentle Jesus . . ." and then stopped. She opened her eyes and asked, "Have you ever met Jesus? Mommy says some people killed him. Why did they do that?" She was obviously thinking about what she was praying, so we discussed the questions for a while before she resumed her prayers. If I had felt the questions were irrelevant, I would have told her to wait until later. We need to use our judgment, to be flexible and open to the guidance of the Holy Spirit in helping a child learn about prayer.

As the children become older, you could introduce them to many of the techniques described in this book, such as cries, one-liners, media prayer, letters to God, poetry and song, and the scrapbook. You could also introduce some of the meditations on concrete themes, such as Reflecting on Nature, The Rosary, The Time Machine, and short periods of contemplation. The youngster's prayer time should be a positive, enjoyable experience, and not treated as a chore or punishment. It is important that children realize that their prayers are between them and God, and that the aim is not to please you. Avoid exploiting the prayer time to pry into their lives or control them. Their relationship with God is private and sacred.

Whatever prayer instruction you give, children will almost certainly learn more from your example than what you say about prayer. *More is caught than taught.* If you neglect your own prayer life, don't be surprised when your children drop the habit and treat it as kid stuff. So be open with them about your spiritual life. Share your own prayer experiences—the joys as well as the difficulties and doubts. Then children and adults can learn from each other and you can all grow in your prayer life together.

GROUP PRAYER

If prayer is an intimate relationship between you and God, why should you pray with other Christians?

When we pray together, we are recognizing that we are not isolated individuals but members of the family of God, headed by Christ. Jesus emphasized this when he said, "Where two or three meet in my name, I shall be there with them" (Mt 18:20). We can learn from each other while giving and receiving support and encouragement. Many of us find it easier to pray together than alone, since we are making a commitment to the group as well as to God.

Almost all local churches have prayer groups. If you don't already belong to a group, find out from your church what is available and see if you can make a trial visit. Many groups have specialized interests, such as healing and intercession, the rosary, charismatic renewal, Christian yoga, or foreign missions. Others combine prayer with study, while some have special requirements for membership. You might look to places of work as well, since many firms, hospitals, colleges, and other organizations have their own prayer groups. If nothing suitable is available, consider organizing your own.

Approach those who you think might be interested, and decide upon a convenient time and place. At your first meeting you will need to establish some ground rules. How often will you meet? Do you want to include study in addition to prayer? Should each meeting have a central theme? Would you like to socialize and serve refreshments? Whom else could you invite to the group? Would you prefer to limit the size? Who will perform the administrative duties? Is there to be a definite attendance requirement? How many weeks or months will the group continue? How would you like the meeting to be structured?

There are basically three ways to run a prayer meeting—as a quiet time together, as a leaderless group, or as a directed meeting. A quiet time together will enable everyone in the group to pray or meditate in silence. This is especially suitable for prayers that can't be shared or said aloud, such as prayers of contemplation, and when people of divergent backgrounds and faiths make up the group.

In a leaderless group, members have an equal opportunity to pray, although one person might be designated to signal the beginning and end of the session. Members can participate at random, or according to some order. Either way, it is advisable that whoever is praying use an agreed upon phrase, such as "Thanks be to God!" or "Amen!" to signal the end of his or her prayer. In random participation, some might pray several times during the meeting, while others could remain silent. It is important that the members are sensitive to each other. Without this awareness, those who are confident at speaking in public or those who want to unload their personal problems could dominate. On occasion people will begin to pray at the same time. When this happens, courtesy should prevail and one person should yield. At other times there may be periods of extended silence when no one will be praying out loud. The members need to appreciate the value of this silence and not feel compelled to fill the void.

A more ordered leaderless style could be described as *domino prayer*, since each member contributes in turn. This works best when the group is arranged in a circle, as it avoids confusion about whose turn is next. One person begins to pray, and after he or she ends with a signal word or phrase, the member on the right (or left) continues, and so on around the circle. Anyone who does not care to offer a prayer need only give the concluding signal. Whenever I have introduced domino prayer to those who were reticent about praying in public, nearly everyone has ended up by contributing some kind of prayer, and often we have gone around the circle several times.

The majority of the groups are directed: they have an appointed leader and a specific program (although sometimes the leadership can revolve among the members). The leader should take into account the age, interests, and social and educational background of the members in planning a program. It would be inappropriate, for instance, to schedule a fifteen minute silent meditation for a class of fidgety school children. This may seem an elementary point, but it is frequently overlooked.

The group leader could select a theme and consider the most effective way of presenting it. Many of the methods suggested in this book can be adapted for group use—letters to God, media prayer, poetry and song, the rosary, Christian yoga, and guided meditations using The Time Machine, the Close-Up, Reflecting on Nature, and possibly the Salesian and Sulpician methods, or contemplation. The leader might take advantage of such audio-visual aids as movie and slide projectors, tape recorders, and blackboards. I have frequently shown religious paintings and objects from nature as the basis for group meditation. I have also used slides of the hungry, the ill, and the dying during prayers of intercession.

One prayer technique which is popular with many prayer leaders is for the members of the group to be asked for their prayer requests so that the leader can include these in his or her prayers on behalf of the group. This method has the advantage of enabling individuals, especially in large groups and congregations, to make a contribution to the prayers where they might otherwise be too shy or not be given the opportunity to pray out loud. Usually the requests are for specific prayers of thanksgiving and intercession—Peter who has a broken leg, thanks for Ethel's successful surgery, Doris and John who are having marital difficulties, Ruth who has an important job interview this week, the students of the parish who are about to take exams. Many churches have a box or some other place where these written prayer requests can be deposited. This enables those who have made the request to stay anonymous.

Leaders should make certain that they are really leading the group in prayer. How often have we been subjected to prayer meetings where the persons in charge treated us as eavesdroppers on their private devotions, put on a show for our entertainment, transformed the group into a therapy session, or turned prayer into a sermon? I remember hearing one television preacher praying, "Lord, you and I know that your people out there have money to spare. But they are holding back on you, Lord. I know that, and you know that. Soften their hearts so that they may give of their abundance to your great work." Needless to say, I did not reach for my checkbook. This pulpiteer wasn't praying; he was sermonizing.

From time to time we hear prayers for the success of a political party in an election, a favorite team in the Super Bowl, a particular church activity which we might consider to be unnecessary and a waste of church funds, or some military venture. What can you do if you disagree with these prayers made on your behalf? Bear in mind that they are offered to God, and he will answer them in his own way. Mention to him how you disagree and ask for his guidance. Then, if the opportunity arises, consider discussing your perspective with those in the group with whom you disagree.

Whatever style of leadership you settle on, it is advisable to have someone pray at the beginning for the Holy Spirit's guidance, perhaps lead you in the Lord's Prayer, and then end in a suitable conclusion like this one of St. Paul: "The grace of the Lord Jesus Christ, the love of God and the fellowship of the Holy Spirit be with you (us) all" (2 Cor 13:13).

PRAYER PARTNERS

There's something to be said for the adage, "The family that prays together stays together." While prayer is not marital glue, couples who pray together usually find that their relationship to God and to each other is strengthened. They can support each other and together they can bring God their special experiences and concerns.

Although your spouse would be an obvious choice, you don't have to be married or limit yourself to one prayer partner. You could consider including your immediate family, a relative, close friend, roommate, or someone who is unable to leave home. In this way, the shut-in will feel less isolated spiritually, and both your lives will be enriched. You need only have a common desire to share in prayer.

The methods for prayer partners are akin to those for prayer groups. You will need to establish guidelines as to when, where, what, and how you are going to pray. You also need to decide whether you plan to combine study with prayer, and whether this will supplement your private devotions or constitute your main prayer time. You could choose to pray silently together, perhaps while joining hands, as you offer your separate prayers to God. Either decide on a pre-determined length of time, or agree upon an unobtrusive signal, such as opening your eyes at the end of your prayers, to let your partner know that you have finished.

Another possibility is to take turns praying aloud. Remember, it is a partnership, not an opportunity for one of you to dominate. This is why my wife and I, who are both strong-willed, prefer to pray in silence. Even if you do pray out loud, you might want to draw the line at sharing your confessions. It could come as a shock if your spouse were to discover during prayer time that you had been fantasizing about having a lustful weekend on a desert island with your next-door neighbor. Far from bringing you closer together, prayer under these circumstances could well have the opposite effect!

A pen pal can also make a good prayer partner. Many have found one through the personal column in religious publications, a church bulletin, or a friendship with someone they met while traveling. In these cases, partners usually correspond by letter or cassette. I have even heard of radio hams having prayer sessions on the air. A pen pal exchange tends to be less of a prayer meeting and more of a discussion of one's spiritual life. But even when separated by geographical distances, the partners are still held together by their common bond of prayer.

SECTION VIII

Companions to Prayer

PROPS AND CUSTOMS

Many Christian denominations have their own prayer customs and aids. While some of these practices such as stations of the cross, novenas, prayer watches, votive candles, and icons have merit, others such as walling up and flagellation are obviously historical curiosities—and that is how they should remain!

Stations of the Cross

This is a series of fourteen scenes depicting Christ's passion, commonly found on the walls of most Roman Catholic and some Anglican (Episcopal) churches. This meditation grew out of the practice of pilgrims to the Holy Land who would retrace the route that Jesus might have taken from Pilate's house to Calvary. The devotion consists of meditations at each of the stations in turn: (1) Jesus is condemned to death, (2) Jesus takes up his cross, (3) Jesus falls the first time, (4) Jesus meets his mother, (5) Simon of Cyrene is forced to carry the cross, (6) Veronica wipes the face of Jesus, (7) Jesus falls the second time, (8) Jesus consoles the women of Jerusalem, (9) Jesus falls the third time, (10) Jesus is stripped of his garments, (11) Jesus is nailed to the cross, (12) Jesus dies on the cross, (13) Jesus' body is taken down, and (14) Jesus is laid in the tomb.

There is a Way of the Cross rosary with each station depicted on its medals, as well as many readily available books and pamphlets with a variety of prayers and meditations to be said at each station. You could choose these prepared devotions, or treat each station as the basis for your own meditations.

Icons

Icons are the sacred pictures of the Eastern Orthodox Church, depicting the life of Jesus, his mother, or the saints. The Holy Spirit was regarded as working through the hands of the artists, who painted in a flat, two-dimensional, stylized manner, to avoid creating "graven images." Sometimes called windows to heaven, icons are pictorial representations of a theological truth and are venerated in the same way as Holy Scripture.

If you have access to an icon, or a picture of an icon, you may want to try this technique. Place yourself in the presence of God and then fix your attention on the icon. What does it depict? Jesus and his mother? One of the saints? The beheading of John the Baptist, or the transfiguration? After studying the scene, think about its symbolism. Certain icons, like Our Lady of Perpetual

Icon

Help, have elaborate symbolism. In this icon, well known to Roman Catholics, the archangels Michael and Gabriel are carrying the instruments of the crucifixion; the Greek letters stand for Mother of God, Jesus Christ, and the archangels, while the gold background represents heaven. The infant Jesus is looking away from his mother toward his mission in the world. This is certainly not intended as a sentimental family portrait but as a visual statement of the incarnation.

After lingering on the symbolic meaning, reflect on its implications for you. Some people feel the message is so clear that the icon "speaks" to them directly.

Sign of the Cross

Since the time of the apostles, many Christians have made the sign of the cross before and after their prayers. This is done by drawing the right hand from the middle of the forehead to the breast, then from the left shoulder to the right, returning to the center, while saying, "In the name of the Father, and of the Son, and of the Holy Spirit. Amen." In the Eastern Church the cross stroke is from right to left. The sign of the cross symbolizes Christ's dying for our sins, and that it is through him that we are offering our prayers.

The Holy Hour

The holy hour—a devotion in honor of Jesus' vigil in the Garden of Gethsemane and his request to his disciples to keep watch for one hour (Mk 14:32–39)—is an opportunity to adore Christ in the Blessed Sacrament for an hour. It is often recommended by spiritual directors as a means to spiritual growth and sanctity. The annual Forty Hours devotion, observed by Roman Catholic parishes, is a longer form, spread over three days, during which the holy sacrament is exposed continuously. On Maundy Thursday, after the sacrament is taken to the altar of repose, it is customary to spend an hour in prayer in its presence, although it is not essential to pass the entire time before the Blessed Sacrament.

Novenas

A novena (from the Latin word for nine) is a series of prayers over nine consecutive days on a special theme or intention to the Holy Spirit, the Sacred Heart of Jesus, or a saint. A novena may be made privately anywhere, or publicly in a church. This devotion traces its origins to the period, traditionally believed to have been nine days, that Mary and the disciples spent between the Ascension and Pentecost (Acts 1:14). Associated mainly with the Roman Catholic Church, novenas provide a framework for extending prayer over many days on a specific theme. Popular novenas include those to St. Anthony, St. Joseph, St. Jude, and St. Anne, as well as many to the Blessed Virgin under her numerous titles—Our Lady of Guadalupe, Our Lady of Perpetual Help, Our Lady of Sorrows, Our Lady of Lourdes, Our Lady of the Miraculous Medal, and the Immaculate Conception.

Votive Candle

Votive Candles

Lighting a candle as an expression of faith began in the eleventh century. It is a custom of the Roman Catholic, Eastern Orthodox, and many Anglican Churches, and is symbolically associated with Christ, the "light of the world" (Jn 8:12). When you light your candle, thank God for the light of Christ and pray that he may work through you and the Church to spread his light into the world. As the flame will continue long after your prayer, pray that you, too, will continue to shine as a witness.

The Angelus

For many Roman Catholics the Angelus prayer is connected with the church bells ringing in early morning, noontime, and evening, especially in southern Europe, as a signal to pray. The word "Angelus" comes from the beginning of the Latin text, "The angel of the Lord announced unto Mary. . . ." In its present form it dates from the early eighteenth century, although its origins go back to nearly four centuries earlier. Over recent years this prayer has been revived as a part of family devotions.

The prayer, in the form of versicles and responses centered around the Hail Mary, is normally said by two or more people.

V. The angel of the Lord announced unto Mary,
R. And she conceived by the Holy Ghost.
V. Hail Mary, full of grace,
    the Lord is with thee;
  blessed art thou amongst women,
    and blessed is the fruit of thy womb, Jesus.
R. Holy Mary, Mother of God,
    pray for us sinners,
    now and at the hour of our death. Amen.
V. Behold the handmaid of the Lord;
R. Be it unto me according to thy word.
V. Hail Mary . . .
R. Holy Mary . . .
V. And the word was made flesh,
R. And dwelt among us.

V. Hail Mary . . .
R. Holy Mary . . .
V. Pray for us, O Holy Mother of God,
R. That we may be made worthy of the promises of Christ.
Let us pray: We beseech thee, O Lord, to pour thy grace into
our hearts: that, as we have known the incarnation of thy Son
Jesus Christ by the message of an angel, so by his cross and
passion, we may be brought unto the glory of the resurrection.
Through the same Christ our Lord. Amen.

Walling Up

This practice began with hermits who withdrew from the world
to lead a solitary life of prayer and penance. They chose to be
permanently enclosed or "walled up" in cells attached to parish
churches.

For instance, in the thirteenth century, a woman hermit named
Verdiana in Tuscany spent thirty-four years in penitential prayer
in a ten by four foot cell. Her only communication with the outside world was a small window in the church wall, through which
she received a little bread and water and occasionally a few vege-
tables.

Your local church is not likely to be very cooperative if you wish
to reinstate this medieval custom!

Flagellation

Flagellation and other means of self-imposed mortification, like
chain mail and hair shirts, came into vogue in medieval times as
an extreme form of penance and a demonstration of one's love of
God.

The thirteenth century hermit, Rainerius Inclusus, who lived in a
cell adjoining the Osnabruck Cathedral for twenty-two years, was
a typical example. He wore chain mail and a hair shirt under his
coarse habit, and flagellated himself regularly until the blood ran.

He believed that his self-torture enabled him to identify with Christ's sufferings.

Even today some people punish themselves before they feel worthy to approach God in prayer. We should emphasize the joy of the resurrection instead of going to extremes in imitating the agonies of Christ's death. After all, he died that we might live.

FASTING

In recent years fasting has been promoted as a quick way to lose weight, make you feel younger and sexier, rid the body of toxins, regulate the bowels, sharpen the senses, and cut grocery bills. It has been used to create empathy with the poor and hungry, to raise funds for various causes, and to protest political wrongs. The suffragettes in England at the beginning of the century went on prison hunger strikes for the women's right to vote, while Gandhi fasted to unite India in resisting British rule.

For the Christian, fasting has traditionally served as an aid to prayer. We choose to deny ourselves nourishment as a symbol of our love and devotion to God so that we might draw closer to him. In a nutshell, *we fast to feast on God.*

This was discovered by a middle aged, lifelong Christian who took a closer look at the ascetic existence of John the Baptist (Mk 1:6; 2:18f), Jesus' forty-day fast in the wilderness (Mt 4:2), and the fasting practices of the Apostles (Acts 13:3; 14:23) and decided to give it a try. "At first I was dubious about fasting," he explained. "The New Testament offers little in the way of practical advice, and fasting has always struck me as being more akin to mortification and hair shirts than a useful prayer tool. To my surprise, it turned out to be more than a diet. I didn't feel as hungry as I thought I would, and it really did facilitate my prayers. I prayed more frequently and felt closer to God than ever before."

There are four types of fasts: partial, traditional, total, and interrupted. In a partial fast only liquid nourishment is taken—juices, milk, broth, and water. This is a good way to begin. After four or five days you could try restricting yourself to water. This is the traditional water fast which can be maintained for periods of several weeks. A total fast means complete abstinence from food and fluids, and cannot be considered safe for more than a day. Muslims practice a variation of this form of fasting during the month of Ramadan, when they take nothing to eat or drink from sunrise to sunset. In an interrupted fast the number of meals is reduced, usually to one a day. You might consider this style of fast during Lent or Advent. Since a lengthy traditional fast is out of the question for most of us who work full time and have family responsibilities, it might be more realistic to consider fasting one day a week.

If you are going to attempt a fast in any form for more than twenty-four hours, be sure to take these precautions:

- Check with your doctor first, and make certain that any medications you are on will not conflict with the fasting program. Generally, fasting is not recommended for children, the elderly, or anyone suffering from heart disease, cancer, bleeding ulcers, gout, liver or kidney disease, juvenile diabetes, or hypoglycemia. It is also not recommended if you are pregnant, very thin, or have a history of anorexia nervosa.
- Diuretics are to be avoided.
- Drink at least two quarts of water daily, preferably mineral water; otherwise take mineral supplements.
- Reduce your physical activities. If you are employed at heavy manual labor or have a job such as an airline pilot where safety is involved, wait for your vacation before attempting a fast.
- The hunger pangs should subside after two or three days. If you are still hungry after four days, or have nausea, consult your doctor. These are danger signs.
- The return to normal eating *must* be made gradually. Follow your doctor's advice for breaking the fast.

Your fast should not be a morbid affair, but a positive experience undertaken out of love for God. It can deepen your prayer life and your commitment to him.

KEEPING IN TOUCH

If you are to have more than a casual acquaintance with God, you will need to develop a dynamic, regular pattern of prayer. You will need to keep in touch.

That means having a definite prayer schedule. You might like to plan yours for a week or a month at a time. Try to allot at least fifteen to twenty minutes twice a day (see *Finding the Time*). During these sessions you could include conversational forms of prayer and the shorter meditations (the close-up, rosary, time machine) or even a brief contemplation, perhaps using the Jesus Prayer or a Christian form of TM. If you plan to meditate on a passage from the Scriptures or other spiritual literature, schedule additional time for the reading. Don't let your books become a substitute for prayer.

As most of us are hard pressed for time during the week, the lengthier Salesian and Sulpician meditations, or in-depth contemplation, could be reserved for the weekends or special times during the Church year, such as Lent. Periodically, for the sake of variety, you might choose to write a letter to God, update your scrapbook, or make an excursion to the countryside to reflect on nature. Try to take time for a yearly retreat so that you can get away from your usual surroundings to take stock of and renew your spiritual life. Weekly or Lenten fasts might also figure in your program.

It can be worthwhile spending a little time writing out an agenda for your meeting with God. It needn't be long or highly structured—just a few notes so that you are thinking about how you approach God and how you can best use your prayer time.

Remember to begin each prayer session by placing yourself in God's presence and asking for his guidance. Don't forget to allow a period of silence for God to speak to you. Here are typical examples of how Mary Macdonald and I have each spent a twenty minute prayer time.

On this occasion, Mary's morning prayers were centered around the rosary:

1. Offering herself, her prayers, and the day to God, using her own adaptation of the traditional Catholic Morning Offering.
2. A request for strength and direction in the concerns and problems she was facing, followed by some moments of silence.
3. Intercessions at the beginning of the rosary.
4. A meditation on one mystery of the rosary with prayers flowing from the associations.

My evening prayers, on the other hand, were more tightly structured:

1. A warm up to place myself in the presence of God, followed by a period of silence.
2. A self-examination and confession of sin.
3. Thanksgiving for God's guidance in my life and asking for his assistance the following day.
4. Prayers for my family, the Church, and Christian mission.
5. A close-up meditation on one of the Beatitudes with a request to obtain that virtue.
6. Another period of silence.
7. The Lord's Prayer.

There are many possible combinations. But however varied and interesting a prayer menu you have created, be ready to drop your prepared program if you feel you are being led in a different direction by the Holy Spirit.

A common mistake of newcomers to prayer is being initially so fired with enthusiasm that that they spend hours on their knees, setting a pace which is hard to maintain. Not surprisingly their fervor soon abates. It is preferable to reverse the process by beginning with realistic expectations and gradually extending the prayer program.

Try to set aside a time, perhaps once a month, for review and evaluation of your prayer life. If you have written agendas, save them along with any comments you have made and make this the basis of a personal prayer log. After reading through your entries for the month, ask yourself questions like these:

- In what way did God reveal himself to me during prayer?
- Am I allowing time to listen to God?
- How did my prayers have an impact on my daily life?
- Were they mainly God-centered, self-centered, or other-centered?
- Have I been honest with God or is there something I am trying to hide?
- Have I been offering to God all the gifts he has given me— my abilities, possessions, and time?
- Are there people who need my prayers whom I have left out?
- Have I become more interested in the prayer technique than the encounter with God?
- Do I look forward to my prayer times? If not, what positive steps can I take?
- What difficulties did I encounter? Do I need to pray in a quieter place, use a different prayer technique, do more spiritual reading, or discuss the problems with a spiritual director?
- Am I self-satisfied and proud of my spiritual prowess?
- Did I carry out the resolutions I made?
- Am I reflecting God's love to others?

Your evaluations should give you some practical ideas on how to improve your prayer life so that you can develop a deep and lasting relationship with God.

THE SPIRITUAL DIRECTOR

When the disciples wanted to learn how to pray, they asked Jesus to teach them. They realized that prayer is like any other skill. It helps to have a good teacher. In the same way, we, too, can profit from the guidance of a spiritual director or soul friend—a devout Christian with whom we can share our spiritual experiences and gain insight and guidance. Such a friend can encourage and extend us, as well as help us to avoid pitfalls such as expecting instant results, overextending ourselves, going off on tangents, or becoming distracted or discouraged.

Many of us tend to treat spiritual direction like marriage counseling: we resort to it at the eleventh hour when our spiritual lives are on the verge of collapse. We can view our prayer life as a private affair with God, and become so subjectively involved that we are not in the best position to take a dispassionate view of our spiritual development. But although our communications with him are personal, we need to recognize that we are members of the body of Christ and that the Holy Spirit can work through others who have the gift of instruction (1 Cor 12:8).

Spiritual direction should not be confused with psychotherapy, other forms of counseling, or even sacramental confession. You might choose to combine your director and confessor, but be aware that someone competent in one field might not be strong in the other. Since the relationship you will have with your spiritual director is akin to that between an apprentice and a master, you will need to look for someone who leads a devout life, with whom you have empathy, and in whom you can trust. He or she should be adept at helping to increase spiritual awareness, and preferably have the same prayer focus as you—be it contempla-tion, the Jesus Prayer, Christian yoga, or the meditation methods. It is advisable to select someone who is flexible, sensitive, and perceptive and can tailor the program to your needs.

Good spiritual directors don't usually advertise their services. They are distinguished by their humility, which makes them hard to find. Begin by praying that the Holy Spirit will guide you in your search. Then consult other Christians for their advice, or check with your local church. A major source of spiritual direc-tors is retreat houses and religious orders—especially the Jesuits, Dominicans and Augustinians—which usually welcome anyone seeking guidance. Don't restrict your sights to your own religious circle or denomination. Remember, too, that many excellent spir-itual directors are to be found among the laity. The Anglican writer, Evelyn Underhill, received direction from a German Catholic layman, Baron von Hügel.

Gifted directors usually have full appointment books, so be pa-tient. Once you have located a likely person, arrange a prelimi-nary meeting to see if a working relationship is possible. Inquire about the director's approach: is it tightly structured with a step by step procedure, or mostly discussion of your spiritual experi-ences? How does the director accept opinions that diverge from his or her own? Conversely, could you accept advice? Is there a free exchange of ideas? Do you feel confident in his or her abili-ty?

If you feel uneasy, don't be afraid to mention this. It is far better to recognize any incompatibility at this stage than later. Like-wise, the director also needs a chance to determine if he or she could help you spiritually. When you have settled on a director, decide on the times you will meet and try to commit yourself ini-tially for a year.

Unlike other forms of counseling, most spiritual directors do not charge for their services. But unless your advisor is from your own parish, it is appropriate to give a donation to the church or the religious order concerned.

RETREATS

All of us could benefit from setting aside some time, at least once a year, to take stock, refresh ourselves, and have an in-depth period with God. For most, this will mean a weekend or a few days during vacation, spent at a retreat center, a monastery or convent, a camp, or even at home. Retreat houses are often situated in beautiful surroundings to help us unwind and leave our daily cares behind. One I went to in the desert near Palm Springs even had a swimming pool and a jacuzzi!

There are various types of retreats. Before you sign up for one, find out how it will be run. Most are conducted in groups and consist of conferences, discussion periods, and time for meditation on assigned readings. There is usually the option of a personal appointment with the retreat conductor, as well as leisure time. The heart of a retreat is the daily worship services, which may include the Eucharist as well as morning, mid-day, and evening prayer, and compline. Sometimes the retreatants are expected to maintain silence throughout the retreat or else during designated periods in order to be alone with God.

Besides a group retreat, you might consider an individually directed one. Some retreat centers, especially those run by the Cenacle Sisters, the Jesuits, and the Dominicans, provide for personalized spiritual direction. In Benedictine and Anglican (Episcopal) houses, which are usually operated as part of a working monastery or convent, you will often be free to join in their Eucharist and daily offices.

The majority of conducted retreats are based on a theme, such as spiritual healing, contemplation, charismatic renewal, journal writing, or the Scriptures. Some groups, like Alcoholics Anonymous, the separated and divorced, married couples, religious education teachers, and lay readers, will have specialized themes. Check to see what is available and inquire if there are any specific conditions. Some retreat centers will admit only men or only women. Others do not welcome families with small children. Write or phone ahead for specific information, costs, and reservations. Retreat houses gladly accept donations and may make special arrangements for those in genuine financial need.

Further information can be found in the annual Catholic Almanac and the Directory of Religious Communities of the Anglican Church in the Americas.

If you can't get away for an organized retreat, you might consider a day or weekend retreat at home, in a vacation spot, or at a local church. Wherever you are, try to avoid interruptions by alerting your family and friends and taking the phone off the hook. Map out a general program in advance, if possible on a theme, and allow for varied activities as well as breaks for food and relaxation. Have available your Bible and other spiritual reading along with a prayer book with services of morning and evening prayer. Your program might look like this:

Morning

- Rise early and say prayers of adoration, thanksgiving, and confession. (You might prefer to do an extensive self-examination and sacramental confession the day before.)
- If there is an early service at a local church, you could include this; otherwise, say the office of morning prayer at home.
- Light breakfast.
- Spiritual reading (choose material from the Scriptures, the *Imitation of Christ,* or the life of a devout person, which will serve as a preparation for your meditation period).
- Spend an hour in meditation using one of the methods described in this book.

- Sit in a chair and listen to music, or relax in some other way.
- Light lunch.

Afternoon

- Try writing a letter or a poem to God, or imagine his presence while you speak to him.
- Make your requests to God: think of his creation, the problems of the world, and the needs of your Church, family and friends, as well as your own special needs.
- Spend about half an hour in contemplation.
- Take a walk in the garden or a local park, or relax in another way.
- Light supper

Evening

- Spiritual reading.
- A short period of contemplation
- End the day with a general thanksgiving and evening prayer (evensong, vespers, or compline).

A more austere form of quiet day is the *poustinia*, from the Russian word for desert. The idea here is to spend the day living like a hermit with only tea (or water) and bread. Seclude yourself in a bare room (with possibly a crucifix or icon), away from distractions and intrusions of the outside world, with only your Bible as a companion.

This experience of intense and concentrated prayer can only serve to make you more receptive to God.

SECTION IX

Obstacles to Prayer

OBSTACLES TO PRAYER

It is inevitable that you will run into difficulties from time to time in your prayer life. Here is a convenient check list of the common problems and some suggested remedies you might like to try.

If you don't feel in the right mood to pray . . .
If you wait for the "right" mood, you might never get around to praying. Try to pray regularly even if you feel that you are having an off day. Once you begin, you will probably feel more positive about meeting God. If you reach a stage where your motivation is almost nil, try joining a prayer group or praying with a friend.

If you are apprehensive about approaching God . . .
It is natural to feel a certain amount of awe when we approach our Creator and Sustainer—especially when we think about our sins. But don't be bashful. Accept that God loves you whatever your shortcomings, and that, through Christ, God will forgive you. If you cannot accept this forgiveness, consider making your confession in the presence of a priest or receiving spiritual counsel from a minister. If it is a question of a rift with a friend, take steps to become reconciled.

If you are angry with God . . .
Instead of sulking, tell him about your anger. Let him know why you feel so hurt. God can take it. He has a good self-image!

If God appears abstract and nebulous . . .
Perhaps your approach to God is a little too academic. You could be thinking of God on a cosmic scale, rather than of the one who died out of love for us on the cross. Try responding with love. You

could also address your prayers to Jesus while imagining him present, or try a contemplative method by which you might come to have a direct experience of God within you.

If you suspect that God might not be listening to you . . .
Are you really listening to *him?* Your conversations might seem one-way because they are. You could also be going through a dry spell, during which you are being prepared for God's answer.

If you have doubts about whether God even exists . . .
Remember that St. Thomas, the apostle, was a doubter also. Bring your doubts before God and seek answers to your questions through spiritual reading and counsel.

If you don't know what to say to God . . .
You don't have to say much. You could contemplate him in quietness. You could also pray one-liners throughout the day or use a prayer book or a structured meditation like the rosary.

Once you begin to pray, you are easily distracted . . .
You might need to pray in a different place or adopt a different position. Did you go through a warm-up to prepare yourself for prayer? You could offer your distractions to God and leave them with him. If you are distracted during contemplation, try a centering word, the Jesus Prayer, or move to another form of prayer.

If some of the excitement has gone out of your prayer life . . .
You cannot expect an emotional high every time you pray. Your aim should be developing a mature, ongoing relationship with God rather than striving for consolations and pleasant feelings.

If you find prayer boring . . .
Are you allowing God to challenge you? You might be going through the motions of prayer without opening yourself to the Holy Spirit. Perhaps you need to vary your approach, try a different technique, or alter your prayer schedule.

If you think God isn't answering your requests . . .
Are you expecting instant results or a spectacular miracle? You might also be looking for "yes" answers all the time. God some-

times says no. Have you offered yourself to God so that the Holy Spirit can act through you to help answer your request?

If you are uncertain about his answer . . .
Ask God for clarification and seek the counsel of other Christians.

If you feel that God is imposing on you . . .
God is like that: the more you pray to him, the more he is likely to get you to do for him. After all, that is the point of the first commandment.

Does it matter which technique you use?
It is a question of finding the best way for you to communicate with God. That should be your only criterion. If you are having problems in any area of prayer, seek the help of a spiritual director. If in doubt, stay with the techniques that give you less trouble.

APPENDIX I
ADVICE FROM THE NEW
TESTAMENT ON PRAYER

"But I say this to you: love your enemies and pray for those who persecute you" (Mt 5:44).

"And when you pray, do not imitate the hypocrites: they love to say their prayers standing up in the synagogues and at the street corners for people to see them. I tell you solemnly, they have had their reward. But when you pray, go to your private room and, when you have shut your door, pray to your Father who is in that secret place, and your Father who sees all that is done in secret will reward you" (Mt 6:5–6).

"In your prayers do not babble as the pagans do, for they think that by using many words they will make themselves heard. Do not be like them; your Father knows what you need before you ask him. So you should pray like this:
    Our Father in heaven,
    may your name be held holy,
    your kingdom come,
    your will be done,
    on earth as in heaven.
    Give us today our daily bread.
    And forgive us our debts,
    as we have forgiven those who are in debt to us.
    And do not put us to the test,
    but save us from the evil one.

Yes, if you forgive others their failings, your heavenly Father will forgive you yours; but if you do not forgive others, your Father will not forgive your failings either" (Mt 6:7–15).

"Ask, and it will be given to you; search, and you will find; knock, and the door will be opened to you. For the one who asks always receives; the one who searches always finds; the one who knocks will always have the door opened to him" (Mt 7:7–8).

"I tell you solemnly once again, if two of you on earth agree to ask anything at all, it will be granted to you by my Father in heaven. For where two or three meet in my name, I shall be there with them" (Mt 18:19–20).

"And if you have faith, everything you ask for in prayer you will receive" (Mt 21:22).

"I tell you solemnly, if anyone says to this mountain, 'Get up and throw yourself into the sea,' with no hesitation in his heart but believing that what he says will happen, it will be done for him. I tell you therefore: everything you ask and pray for, believe that you have it already, and it will be yours. And when you stand in prayer, forgive whatever you have against anybody, so that your Father in heaven may forgive your failings too" (Mk 11:23–25).

"You should be awake, and praying not to be put to the test" (Mk 14:38).

"Love your enemies, do good to those who hate you, bless those who curse you, pray for those who treat you badly" (Lk 6:27–28).

"Say this when you pray:
    Father, may your name be held holy,
    your kingdom come;
    give us each day our daily bread,
    and forgive us our sins,
    for we ourselves forgive each one who is in debt to us.
    And do not put us to the test" (Lk 11:2–4).

". . . pray continually and never lose heart" (Lk 18:1).

"Two men went up to the temple to pray, one a Pharisee, the other a tax collector. The Pharisee stood there and said this prayer to himself, 'I thank you, God, that I am not grasping, unjust, adulterous like the rest of mankind, and particularly that I am not like this tax collector here. I fast twice a week; I pay tithes on all I get.' The tax collector stood some distance away, not daring even to raise his eyes to heaven; but he beat his breast and said, 'God, be merciful to me, a sinner.' This man, I tell you, went home again at rights with God; the other did not. For everyone who exalts himself will be humbled, but the man who humbles himself will be exalted" (Lk 18:10–14).

"Whatever you ask for in my name I will do, so that the Father may be glorified in the Son" (Jn 14:13).

"If you remain in me and my words remain in you, you may ask what you will and shall get it" (Jn 15:7).

"Ask and you will receive, and so your joy will be complete" (Jn 16:24).

"The Spirit too comes to help us in our weakness. For when we cannot choose words in order to pray properly, the Spirit himself expresses our plea in a way that could never be put into words, and God who knows everything in our hearts knows perfectly well what he means, and the pleas of the saints expressed by the Spirit are according to the mind of God" (Rom 8:26–27).

"Do not give up if trials come; and keep on praying" (Rom 12:12).

"Anybody with the gift of tongues speaks to God, but not to other people; because nobody understands him when he talks in the spirit about mysterious things" (1 Cor 14:2).

"Since you aspire to spiritual gifts, concentrate on those which will grow to benefit the community. That is why anybody who has the gift of tongues must pray for the power of interpreting them. For if I use this gift in my prayers, my spirit may be praying but my mind is left barren" (1 Cor 14:12–14).

"Pray all the time, asking for what you need, praying in the Spirit on every possible occasion. Never get tired of staying awake to pray for all the saints . . ." (Eph 6:18).

"There is no need to worry; but if there is anything you need, pray for it, asking God for it with prayer and thanksgiving, and that peace of God, which is so much greater than we can understand, will guard your hearts and your thoughts, in Christ Jesus" (Phil 4:6–7).

"Be persevering in your prayers and be thankful as you stay awake to pray. Pray for us especially, asking God to show us opportunities for announcing the message and proclaiming the mystery of Christ, for the sake of which I am in chains; pray that I may proclaim it as clearly as I ought" (Col 4:2–4).

"Be happy at all times; pray constantly; and for all things give thanks to God, because this is what God expects you to do in Christ Jesus" (1 Thes 5:16–18).

"My advice is that, first of all, there should be prayers offered for everyone—petitions, intercessions and thanksgiving—and especially for kings and others in authority, so that we may be able to live religious and reverent lives in peace and quiet" (1 Tim 2:1–2).

"In every place, then, I want the men to lift their hands up reverently in prayer, with no anger or argument" (1 Tim 2:8).

"If any one of you is in trouble, he should pray; if anyone is feeling happy, he should sing a psalm. If one of you is ill, he should send for the elders of the church, and they must anoint him with oil in the name of the Lord and pray over him. The prayer of faith will save the sick man and the Lord will raise him up again; and if he has committed any sins, he will be forgiven. So confess your sins to one another, and pray for one another, and this will cure you; the heartfelt prayer of a good man works very powerfully" (Jas 5:13–16).

"... if we cannot be condemned by our own conscience we need not be afraid in God's presence, and whatever we ask him, we shall receive, because we keep his commandments and live the kind of life he wants" (1 Jn 3:21–22).

"We are quite confident that if we ask him for anything, and it is in accordance with his will, he will hear us; and, knowing that whatever we may ask, he hears us, we know that we have already been granted what we asked of him" (1 Jn 5:14–15).

APPENDIX II
SOME TRADITIONAL PRAYER
METHODS IN OUTLINE

Making Decisions

1. Pray for God's guidance.
2. Set out the pros and cons of each alternative.
3. Evaluate and list them in terms of your goals in life.
4. Assume that you have made a decision, and imagine how you would react to each alternative.
5. Pray for God's direction.
6. Seek counsel, if still in doubt.

The Time Machine

1. Choose a story you can visualize from the Scriptures or the lives of the saints, and imagine the scene as a participant or an observer.
2. Consider the main points of the story.
3. Think about how they apply to you.
4. What practical course of action can you take?
5. Pray for God's guidance in forming a resolution and carrying it out.

Reflecting on Nature

1. Examine an object in detail.
2. Think about its functions.
3. Thank God, and ask for direction in using his creation.
4. Consider possible symbolic associations.

5. Pray that the Holy Spirit will show you what you can learn from nature.
6. What course of action do your reflections suggest?

Salesian Devotion

1. Choose a meditation theme.
2. Place yourself in the presence of God.
3. Ask for God's assistance in the meditation.
4. Imagine you are there (if you can do this with the topic).
5. Select one or two points for reflection.
6. Allow the reflections to open your heart to God.
7. Form specific resolutions.
8. Thank God for the meditation, and ask him to bless your resolution.
9. Select a few points as your spiritual bouquet.

The Method of St. Peter of Alcantara (1499–1562)

Although this method was not included in the text, because of similarities with other techniques, its outline is given here as an alternative. It is a complete meditation/prayer method, designed for periods of one and a half hours or more.

1. Make the sign of the cross.
2. Examine your life, and confess your sins.
3. Ask for the Holy Spirit's guidance in your meditation.
4. Read a short passage for meditation.
5. Either imagine you are there at the scene, or let the significance of the theological truth open your heart and mind to God.
6. Make a specific thanksgiving to God for the meditation as well as a general one for what he has done for you.
7. Offer yourself and all you have to God.
8. Make prayers of petition and intercessions.

Sulpician Approach

1. The night before, select one of Jesus' virtues as your meditation subject.

2. Begin your meditation by placing yourself in God's presence.
3. Ask the Holy Spirit to guide you in your meditation.
4. Adore in Jesus the virtue which you have chosen as your meditation subject.
5. Consider your own lack of this virtue, and open yourself to receiving it.
6. Resolve to put this virtue into practice.
7. Thank God for the grace he has given you.
8. Choose a few points for your spiritual bouquet.

FURTHER READING

General

Alphonsus Liguori, St. *How To Converse Continually and Familiarly with God*. Tr. by L.X. Aubin. Boston: St. Paul Editions, n.d. St. Alphonsus urges us toward greater intimacy with God, sharing with him all our concerns in trust and love as though talking with a dearest friend.

Basset, Bernard. *Let's Start Praying Again*. Garden City, N.Y.: Image, 1973. A partly autobiographical overall approach underscoring the joy of prayer.

Bloom, Anthony. *Beginning To Pray*. New York: Paulist Press, 1970. In these chapters, originally given as talks to people who had never prayed, Russian Orthodox Archbishop Anthony Bloom considers the apparent absence of God, knocking at the door, and going inward through prayer.

Bloom, Anthony. *Living Prayer*. Springfield, Illinois: Templegate, 1966. Contains an original interpretation of the Lord's Prayer. Beginning at the end of the prayer and working forward, Bloom traces the ascent of the soul from bondage to freedom.

Calvin, Jean. *Institutes of the Christian Religion*. Vols. 20 and 21 of The Library of Christian Classics. Ed. by John T. McNeill; tr. by Ford Lewis Battles. Philadelphia: Westminster Press, 1960. Includes a detailed analysis of the Lord's Prayer.

Carretto, Carlo. *Letters from the Desert*. Tr. by Rose Mary Hancock with a Foreword by Ivan Illich. Maryknoll, N.Y.: Orbis, 1975. In this international bestseller, Carretto writes of prayer and his call to the solitary life as a Little Brother in the Sahara.

Catoir, John. *Enjoy the Lord: A Path to Contemplation.* New York: Christophers, 1978. A practical guide to prayer with an interesting chapter on how other Christians have prayed.

Chervin, Ronda. *Prayer and Your Everyday Life.* Liguori, Missouri: Liguori Publications, 1975. This booklet, written with a charismatic emphasis, contains useful prayer exercises.

Coburn, John B. *Prayer and Personal Religion.* Philadelphia: Westminster Press, 1957. This helpful basic book by an Episcopalian bishop includes prayer groups, spiritual reading, and retreats.

Heffner, Christine Fleming. *Intercession: The Greatest Service.* West Park, N.Y.: Holy Cross Publications, 1967. Practical suggestions on intercession—devotional, sacramental, and sacrificial—with a short chapter on group prayer.

Heyer, Robert (ed.). *How Do I Pray?* New York: Paulist Press, 1977. Twenty-eight Christians, both clergy and laity, answer the question: How do I pray?

Huntington, James. *The Work of Prayer.* Cincinnati: Forward Movement, 1975. Some thoughts on prayer—our relationship to God, forming a habit or rule of prayer, and learning to pray from the Lord's Prayer—discussed by the founder of the Episcopal Order of the Holy Cross.

Jungmann, Joseph A. *Christian Prayer Through the Centuries.* Tr. by John Coyne. New York: Paulist Press, 1978. A fascinating review of the habits of prayer from apostolic times up to the nineteenth century.

Lekeux, Martial. *The Art of Prayer.* Tr. by Paul Joseph Oligny. Chicago: Franciscan Herald Press, 1974. A comprehensive traditional manual more suited for religious than laity.

Link, Mark. *You: Prayer for Beginners and Those Who Have Forgotten How.* Niles, Illinois: Argus Communications, 1976. A seven week program that covers conversational prayer, meditation, contemplation, journal writing, spiritual reading, and forty-nine guided prayer experiences.

Lohmeyer, Ernst. *"Our Father": An Introduction to the Lord's Prayer.* Tr. by John Bowden. New York: Harper & Row, 1965. A study on the original texts and historical background of the Lord's Prayer.

Nouwen, Henri J.M. *With Open Hands.* Notre Dame, Indiana: Ave Maria Press, 1977. Nouwen impresses upon us the need to be open, stripping away all defenses and excuses, in order to be fully responsive to God.

Parker, William R., and Elaine St. Johns. *Prayer Can Change Your Life: Experiments and Techniques of Prayer Therapy.* New York: Cornerstone Library/Simon and Schuster, 1980. A unique experiment to test the effectiveness of prayer using scientific research techniques.

Sauvé, Paul. *Petals of Prayer: Creative Ways to Pray.* Locust Valley, N.Y.: Living Flame Press, 1974. Many paths to God are outlined in this guide to prayer: phrase by phrase meditation, spiritual reading, Carmelite, Ignatian, and Sulpician approaches, ejaculatory prayer, the rosary, stations of the cross, and the Jesus Prayer.

Society of St. Margaret. (Written anonymously by a sister.) *Schools of Spirituality: Sketches of the Lives and Thought of Twelve Great Teachers of Christian Spirituality.* West Park, N.Y.: Holy Cross Publications, 1967. Profiles of the spiritual lives of such Christians as St. Augustine, Juliana of Norwich, St. Francis of Assisi, St. Ignatius, St. Teresa, St. Francis de Sales, Charles de Foucauld, and Evelyn Underhill.

Wedge, Florence. *The Lord's Prayer.* Pulaski, Wisconsin: Franciscan Publishers, 1974. An examination of the meaning of each of the seven petitions of the Lord's Prayer with scriptural, historical, and theological insights.

Whiston, Charles F. *Instruction in the Life of Prayer.* Cincinnati: Forward Movement, 1972. A traditional approach to prayer: adoration, self-oblation, petition, daily prayer, sin, acts of devotion, and spiritual direction.

Meditation

Bergewisch, Fred F. *A Rosary for Our Times.* Cincinnati: St. Anthony Messenger, n.d. A booklet of brief meditations on the fifteen rosary mysteries and what they can mean to us.

Boylan, Eugene. *Difficulties in Mental Prayer.* New York: Paulist Press, 1966. A reaction to the formalism of meditation of the last century in favor of more affective communication with God.

De Mello, Anthony. *Sadhana: A Way to God: Christian Exercises in Eastern Form*. St. Louis: Institute of Jesuit Sources, 1979. Christian meditation methods—exercises in awareness, fantasy, and devotion—based on Asian and Ignatian techniques.

Francis de Sales, St. *Introduction to the Devout Life*. Tr. and ed. by John K. Ryan. Garden City, N.Y.: Image, 1972. A concise and very readable classic, intended for lay people.

Frost, Bede. *The Art of Mental Prayer*. Milwaukee, Wisconsin: Morehouse, 1931. An extensive survey of historical meditation techniques by an Anglican Benedictine.

Gottemoller, Bartholomew. *How To Find Happiness: A Simple Yet Comprehensive Treatment of Christian Prayer*. Huntington, Indiana: Our Sunday Visitor, 1979. A good introduction to mental prayer and contemplation, with a helpful section on using images of God as Creator, Father, Spouse, and Life, by a Trappist monk with forty-five years' experience.

Habig, Marion A. *The Franciscan Crown*. Chicago: Franciscan Herald Press, 1976. A history of the Franciscan rosary or crown, and meditations on the seven joyful mysteries.

Harrington, Wilfrid J. *The Rosary: A Gospel Prayer*. Canfield, Ohio: Alba, 1975. A Vatican II look at the rosary mysteries in a scriptural and historical perspective.

Harton, F.P. *The Elements of the Scriptural Life: A Study in Ascetical Theology*. London: S.P.C.K., 1957. A major work on prayer and spirituality by an Anglican priest.

Hughson, S.C. *Spiritual Guidance: A Study of the Godward Way*. West Park, N.Y.: Holy Cross Press, 1948. Includes chapters on meditation, affective prayer, and contemplation.

Ignatius of Loyola, St. *The Spiritual Exercises of St. Ignatius*. Tr. by Anthony Mottola with an Introduction by Robert W. Gleason. Garden City, N.Y.: Image, 1964. This classic, intended as a retreat director's manual and presented in somewhat fragmentary form, contains much useful material.

Kelsey, Morton T. *The Other Side of Silence: A Guide to Christian Meditation.* New York: Paulist Press, 1976. Kelsey emphasizes the role of imagery in meditation in an approach strongly influenced by Carl Jung.

Johnson, John S. *The Rosary in Action.* Rockford, Illinois: Tan Books, 1977. Practical suggestions on coordinating the meditations and vocal prayers of the rosary.

LeShan, Lawrence. *How to Meditate: A Guide to Self-Discovery.* New York: Bantam, 1979. A practical guide to meditation, not specifically Christian in emphasis, by a psychotherapist.

Paul VI, John XXIII, and Leo XIII. *Seventeen Papal Documents on the Rosary.* Boston: St. Paul Editions, 1980. Paul VI's pronouncement on devotion to the Blessed Virgin (Marialis Cultus) and John XXIII's meditations on the rosary mysteries are included in this collection of encyclicals and documents.

Peter of Alcantara, St. *A Golden Treatise of Mental Prayer.* Ed. by G.S. Hollings. Chicago: Franciscan Herald Press, 1978. A modern edition of the meditation method of this sixteenth century Spanish Franciscan.

Pipkin, H. Wayne. *Christian Meditation, Its Art and Practice.* New York: Hawthorn, 1977. The author proposes a Christian alternative to Transcendental Meditation, and includes guided meditations, designed for groups.

Tanquerey, Adolphe. *The Spiritual Life: A Treatise on Ascetical and Mystical Theology.* Westminster, Maryland: Newman Bookshop, 1948. The standard text for seminarians on mental prayer and spirituality.

Trobisch, Walter. *Martin Luther's Quiet Time.* Downers Grove, Illinois: InterVarsity Press, 1975. In a forty page letter written to his barber, Martin Luther outlined his own method of meditation. He would consider a short passage as a teaching, thanksgiving, confession of sin, and petition.

Tronson, Louis. *Oeuvres Complètes.* Paris: Migne, 1857. Untranslated treatise on meditation, commonly known as the Sulpician Method, by Fr. Tronson, third Superior General of the Seminary of St. Sulpice.

Willett, Robert F. *Primer for Christian Meditation.* Wilton, Connecticut: Morehouse-Barlow, 1976. Fr. Willett presents a Zen-inspired meditation technique, with a potpourri of unusual prayer ideas, as well as two guided meditations.

Contemplation and Mysticism

Anonymous. *The Cloud of Unknowing and The Book of Privy Counseling.* Ed. with an introduction by William Johnston. Garden City, N.Y.: Image, 1973. This edition of the well read fourteenth century classic includes cross-references to the works of St. John of the Cross.

Brother Lawrence of the Resurrection. *The Practice of the Presence of God.* Tr. by John J. Delaney. Foreword by Henri J.M. Nouwen. Garden City, N.Y.: Image, 1977. A classic by a humble seventeenth century Carmelite lay brother.

Caussade, Jean-Pierre de. *Abandonment to Divine Providence.* Tr. with an Introduction by John Beevers. Garden City, N.Y.: Image, 1975. An eighteenth century work on the importance of total surrender to God.

Chantal, St. Jane Frances de. *St. Chantal on Prayer.* Tr. by Rev. A. Durand. Boston: St. Paul Editions, 1968. A selection from the writings on prayer of St. Chantal, who, under the guidance of her spiritual director, St. Francis de Sales, founded the Order of the Visitation.

Diefenbach, Gabriel. *Common Mystic Prayer.* Boston: St. Paul Editions, 1978. Intended as "a simple statement of the beginnings of mystic prayer," this book also contains a good summary of the spirituality of St. John of the Cross.

Ferguson, James. *An Illustrated Encyclopedia of Mysticism and the Mystery Religions.* New York: Seabury Press, 1977. This reference work, with over one thousand succinct entries, covers Christian and Asian mysticism, the occult, and associated phenomena.

Foucauld, Charles de. *Come, Let Us Sing a Song Unknown: Prayers of Charles de Foucauld.* Denville, New Jersey: Dimension, n.d. First American posthumous edition of the writings of this twentieth century desert hermit, including a meditation on the Lord's Prayer.

Guigo II. *The Ladder of Monks and Twelve Meditations.* Tr. with an Introduction by Edmund Colledge and James Walsh. Garden City, N.Y.: Image, 1978. Guigo, a twelfth century French prior, outlines four steps to union with God. Reading seeks, meditation perceives, prayer asks for, and contemplation tastes the sweetness of mystical union.

Harkness, Georgia. *Mysticism: Its Meaning and Message.* Nashville, Tennessee: Abingdon Press, 1973. An historical overview of Christian mysticism and the major writers, including several of the twentieth century.

Hilton, Walter. *The Stairway of Perfection.* Tr. with an Introduction by M.L. Del Mastro. Garden City, N.Y.: Image, 1979. This fourteenth century work includes a concise explanation of the stages to mystical union.

James, William. *The Varieties of Religious Experience.* New York: Mentor Books, 1958. This classic psychological work contains a short study of mysticism.

John of the Cross, St. *The Collected Works of St. John of the Cross.* Tr. by Kieran Kavanaugh and Otilio Rodriguez. Washington, D.C.: Institute of Carmelite Studies, 1979. Most readable of the available English translations.

Keating, Thomas, M. Basil Pennington and Thomas E. Clark. *Finding Grace at the Center.* Still River, Massachusetts: St. Bede Publications, 1978. Consists of four articles on centering prayer and "Contemplative Prayer in the Christian Tradition: An Historical Perspective" by Abbot Keating.

Knowles, David. *The English Mystical Tradition.* Harper & Row, 1961. Includes the fourteenth century mystics Juliana of Norwich, Walter Hilton, Richard Rolle, and the anonymous author of *The Cloud of Unknowing.*

Merton, Thomas. *New Seeds of Contemplation.* New York: New Directions, 1972. The chapters on contemplation, mental prayer, and distractions are especially helpful.

Peers, E. Allison. *Spanish Mysticism.* New York: E.P. Dutton, n.d. Short studies on the major Spanish mystics.

Pennington, M. Basil. *Centering Prayer: Renewing an Ancient Christian Prayer Form.* Garden City, N.Y.: Doubleday, 1980. Fr. Pennington's most extensive discussion of centering prayer.

Placa, Alan, and Brendan P. Riordan. *Desert Silence: A Way of Prayer for an Unquiet Age.* Locust Valley, N.Y.: Living Flame Press, 1977. The way of prayer of the Desert Fathers, including short meditations on their sayings.

Poslusney, Vernard. *Attaining Spiritual Maturity: According to St. John of the Cross.* Locust Valley, N.Y.: Living Flame Press, 1973. An introduction to the ascetical way of *The Ascent of Mount Carmel* and *The Dark Night.*

Poslusney, Vernard. *The Prayer of Love: The Art of Aspiration.* Locust Valley, N.Y.: Living Flame Press, 1977. Contains a history of the prayer of aspiration, methods of St. Francis de Sales, St. Teresa, and others, and a selection of aspirations from the Bible and other sources.

Poslusney, Vernard. *Union with the Lord in Prayer.* Locust Valley, N.Y.: Living Flame Press, 1978. A description of affective prayer, aspirations, and the prayer of simplicity, or acquired contemplation.

Rolle, Richard. *The Fire of Love and the Mending of Life.* Tr. by M.L. Del Mastro. Garden City, N.Y.: Image, 1981. This fourteenth century English mystic ranks alongside Juliana of Norwich, Walter Hilton, and the unknown author of *The Cloud of Unknowing.*

Teresa of Avila, St. *The Collected Works of St. Teresa of Avila.* Tr. by Kieran Kavanaugh and Otilio Rodriguez. Washington, D.C.: Institute of Carmelite Studies, 1976 and 1980. The most recent edition of her works, Volume I contains *The Book of Her Life, Spiritual Testimonies,* and *Soliloquies,* while Volume II includes *The Way of Perfection, Meditations on the Song of Songs,* and *The Interior Castle.*

Underhill, Evelyn. *Mysticism: A Study in the Nature and Development of Man's Spiritual Consciousness.* New York: Meridian Books, 1960. The survey of mystical writers in the appendix of this monumental work and the extensive bibliography are very useful.

The Jesus Prayer

The Art of Prayer: An Orthodox Anthology. Compiled by Igumen Chariton of Valamo; tr. by E. Kadloubovsky and E.M. Palmer; ed. with an Introduction by Timothy Ware. Boston: Faber and Faber, 1978. A collection of writings on prayer, with one section devoted to the Jesus Prayer.

Unseen Warfare, Being the Spiritual Combat and Path to Paradise of Lorenzo Scupoli as Edited by Nicodemus of the Holy Mountain and Revised by Theophan the Recluse. Tr. into English from Theophan's Russian text by E. Kadloubovsky and G.E.H. Palmer. London: Faber and Faber, 1963. The Russian version contains supplementary material on praying in one's own words, cries to God, and the Jesus Prayer in place of Scupoli's chapters on the intercession of the Virgin Mary and the angels.

Writings from the Philokalia on Prayer of the Heart. Tr. by E. Kadloubovsky and G.E.H. Palmer. Boston: Faber and Faber, 1979. Includes commentaries on the Jesus Prayer by Gregory of Sinai, Simeon the New Theologian, and other Eastern Orthodox writers.

Anonymous: Written by a Byzantine Priest. *Reflections on the Jesus Prayer: A Phrase-by-Phrase Analysis of "The Prayer of the Heart."* Denville, New Jersey: Dimension Books, 1978. Much historical, theological, and scriptural information is woven into this phrase by phrase analysis of the Jesus Prayer. The appendix is a commentary on books for further reading.

Anonymous. *The Way of a Pilgrim and The Pilgrim Continues His Way.* Tr. by Helen Bacovcin. Garden City, N.Y.: Image, 1978. The narrative of an unknown nineteenth century Russian peasant and his quest for a means to uninterrupted communion with God, which he found in the Jesus Prayer.

Ingelsby, Brice. *Pray Without Ceasing: The Jesus Prayer.* Stockbridge, Massachusetts: The Marian Press, 1965. An introduction to *The Way of a Pilgrim,* a word by word analysis of the Jesus Prayer, and a helpful outline summary, written from a Roman Catholic perspective.

Maloney, George A. *Prayer of the Heart.* Notre Dame, Indiana: Ave Maria Press, 1981. A guide to contemplation, based on the Jesus Prayer, the early Fathers, and the spirituality of the Eastern Church.

Ware, Kallistos. *The Power of the Name: The Jesus Prayer in Orthodox Spirituality.* Fairacres, Oxford: SLG Press, 1977. A concise booklet on the historical background, the benefits, and the way of praying the Jesus Prayer in the Eastern Orthodox tradition.

Healing

Häring, Bernard. *Discovering God's Mercy: Confession Helps for Today's Catholic.* Liguori, Missouri: Liguori, 1980. The sacrament of reconciliation or confession is seen as a celebration of God's mercy and a source of peace, healing, and liberation. The author describes the revised rite for individual confession, including an examination of conscience using the Lord's Prayer or the Beatitudes, as well as a communal penance service.

Knight, David M. *Confession Can Change Your Life.* Chicago: Claretian Publications, 1977. A re-examination of confession in the light of Vatican II.

Larsen, Earnest. *Body of Christ.* Canfield, Ohio: Alba, 1976. Fr. Larsen draws on his experience from an active youth ministry to reflect on healing through Christ.

Larsen, Earnest. *How To Understand and Overcome Depression.* Liguori, Missouri: Liguori Publications, 1977. A discussion of the psychological causes of depression and the spiritual answer: prayer.

Leuret, Dr. Francois, and Dr. Henri Bon. *Modern Miraculous Cures: A Documented Account of Miracles and Medicine in the Twentieth Century.* Tr. by A.T. Macqueen and John C. Barry. New York: Farrar, Straus and Cudahy, 1957. Includes information on the officially recognized cures at Lourdes.

Linn, Dennis and Matthew. *Healing of Memories.* New York: Paulist Press, 1974. A practical guide to letting go of past hurts and entering into a healing relationship with Christ. Examines the role of confession in the healing process.

MacNutt, Francis. *Healing.* New York: Bantam, 1979. An extensive coverage of physical and emotional healing, including demonic possession, by a leading charismatic.

Stapleton, Ruth Carter. *The Experience of Inner Healing.* New York: Bantam, 1979. A popular self-help guide drawing on many sources—Jung, Kübler-Ross, Ignatius—and including several pages on healing through meditation.

Praying in Tongues

Christenson, Larry. *Speaking in Tongues.* Foreword by Corrie ten Boom. Minneapolis, Minnesota: Dimension Books, 1974. A look at speaking and praying in tongues from a Protestant viewpoint. Helpful section on how to have a daily quiet time with God.

Kelsey, Morton T. *Tongue Speaking: The History and Meaning of the Charismatic Experience.* New York: Crossroad, 1981. An historical approach to glossolalia from biblical and apostolic times to the twentieth century pentecostal movements. The author, though not a tongue speaker, is sympathetic to the subject.

Kildahl, John P. *The Psychology of Speaking in Tongues.* New York: Harper & Row, 1972. A study by a psychotherapist of the relationship of glossalalia to mental health.

Laurentin, René. *Catholic Pentecostalism.* Tr. by Mathew J. O'Connell. New York: Image, 1978. An objective overview of the Catholic charismatic movement, including speaking in tongues and healing.

Samarin, William J. *Tongues of Men and Angels: The Religious Language of Pentecostalism.* New York: Macmillan, 1972. A linguistic analysis of glossolalia samples.

Asian Meditation Techniques

Bloomfield, Harold H. and Robert B. Kory. *Happiness: The TM Program, Psychiatry and Enlightment.* Introduction by Maharishi Mahesh Yogi. New York: Dawn Press/Simon and Schuster, 1976. A discussion of the benefits of TM.

Daishin Buksbazen, John. *To Forget the Self: An Illustrated Guide to Zen Meditation.* Los Angeles: Zen Center of Los Angeles, 1977. This basic introduction to zazen includes exercises to accustom the body to the sitting postures.

Déchanet, J.M. *Christian Yoga.* New York: Harper and Brothers, 1959. One of the first attempts to combine yoga with Christian prayer. The various elements merge in a personal approach.

Ebon, Martin (ed.) *TM: How To Find Peace of Mind Through Meditation.* New York: New American Library, 1975. A collection of articles on TM as well as Silva Mind Control, Arica, Zen, Kundalini yoga, biofeedback, self-hypnosis, and Christian meditation.

Goleman, Daniel. *Varieties of Meditative Experience.* New York: E.P. Dutton, 1977. A survey of paths to meditation: Christian hesychasm, Patanjali's Ashtanga yoga, Tantric and Kundalini yoga, Hindu Bhakti, Jewish Kabbalah, Sufism, Zen, Tibetan Buddhism, Gurdjieff's Fourth Way, and Krishnamurti's Choiceless Awareness.

Haddon, David. *Transcendental Meditation: A Christian View.* Downers Grove, Illinois: InterVarsity Press, 1977. A critical analysis of TM.

Humphreys, Christmas. *Zen Buddhism.* New York: Macmillan, 1963. An excellent historical background of Zen with a description of its practice.

Iyengar, B.K.S. *Light on Yoga.* Foreword by Yehudi Menuhin. New York: Schocken Books, 1966. A major work on yoga, with over six hundred photographs of postures demonstrated by the author.

Johnston, William. *Christian Zen.* New York: Harper & Row, 1979. A ground-breaking book which approaches Zen in the light of Christian mysticism.

Kadowaki, J.K. *Zen and the Bible: A Priest's Experience.* Tr. by Joan Rieck. Boston: Routledge & Kegan Paul, 1980. Fr. Kadowaki sees striking parallels between Zen monastic life and the Jesuit novitiate, Zen and Ignatian retreats, as well as koans and the paradoxical passages of the Bible.

Lysebeth, André van. *Yoga Self-Taught.* Tr. by Carola Congreve. New York: Harper & Row, 1971. A self-instruction manual of hatha yoga, with illustrations showing the progressive stages of the asanas.

Maloney, George A. *TM and Christian Meditation.* Pecos, New Mexico: Dove Publications, 1976. After surveying several mind expansion techniques, Fr. Maloney opts for the Jesus Prayer as a Christian alternative to TM. Includes a guided meditation.

Schloegl, Irmgard. *The Wisdom of the Zen Masters.* New York: New Directions, 1976. The Introduction is a well presented basic summary of Zen.

Slade, Herbert. *Explorations into Contemplative Prayer.* New York: Paulist Press, 1975. Fr. Slade explains how Patanjali's *Yoga Sutras* have been incorporated into the contemplative program of the Cowley Fathers in Oxford.

Suzuki, D.T. *Zen Buddhism: Selected Writings of D.T. Suzuki*. Ed. by William Barrett. Garden City, N.Y.: Doubleday Anchor, 1956. An introduction to the history and meaning of Zen rather than a practical guide.

Upanishads: Breath of the Eternal. Selected and tr. by Swami Prabhavananda and Frederick Manchester. New York: Mentor Books, 1957. Pre-fifth century B.C. Hindu scriptures.

Watts, Alan. *The Spirit of Zen*. London: John Murray, 1958. U.S. edition, New York, Grove Press. The chapter on the Technique of Zen is especially helpful.

White, John. *Everything You Want to Know about TM—Including How To Do It: A Look at Higher Consciousness and the Enlightenment Industry*. New York: Pocket Books, 1976. Contains a how-to section on the procedures of TM.

Wood, Ernest. *Great Systems of Yoga*. New York: The Citadel Press, 1966. A description of seven forms of yoga, as well as Zen, the Buddhist Noble Way, and Sufi yoga.

Group and Family Prayer

Freer, Harold Wiley and Francis B. Hall. *Two or Three Together: A Manual for Prayer Groups*. New York: Harper & Row, 1954. A practical guide to organizing prayer and meditation groups with a thirty week course outline, including an annotated further reading section.

Ghezzi, Bert, and John Blattner (eds). *Prayer Group Workshop*. Ann Arbor, Michigan: Servant Books, 1979. Twenty-two experienced leaders offer practical advice to charismatic prayer groups.

Knight, David M. *Helps for Family Prayer*. Chicago: Claretian Publications, 1977. A handy booklet abounding in ideas for family prayer and special activities.

Shoemaker, Helen Smith. *Prayer Is Action*. New York: Morehouse-Barlow, 1969. A discussion of the benefits of praying together and suggestions for forming small prayer groups.

Fasting

Cott, Dr. Alan. *Fasting: The Ultimate Diet*. New York: Bantam, 1979. Useful medical advice on fasting, including a diet for breaking a fast.

Dobrzynski, Judith H. *Fasting: A Way to Well-Being.* New York: Sovereign Books, 1979. Includes a chapter on fasting in the religions of the world.

Maloney, George A. *A Return to Fasting.* Pecos, New Mexico: Dove Publications, 1974. A booklet on fasting in the Bible and the early Church, with helpful suggestions based on personal experiences.

Spiritual Direction and Journal Writing

Edwards, Tilden H. *Spiritual Friend: Reclaiming the Gift of Spiritual Direction.* New York: Paulist Press, 1980. An examination of the tradition of spiritual direction, as well as practical considerations: what to look for in a spiritual director, how to be one, and how to prepare those called to this ministry.

Kelsey, Morton T. *Adventure Inward: Christian Growth through Personal Journal Writing.* Minneapolis, Minnesota: Augsburg, 1980. A Jungian approach to keeping a spiritual journal.

Leech, Kenneth. *Soul Friend: The Practice of Christian Spirituality.* Introduction by Henri J.M. Nouwen. New York: Harper & Row, 1977. A review of spiritual direction in Eastern and Western traditions, the roles of director, counselor, and therapist, as well as direction and the sacrament of reconciliation.

Simons, George F. *Keeping Your Personal Journal.* New York: Paulist Press, 1978. An introduction to the methods of journal writing.

Retreats

Book of Common Prayer, The. New York: Seabury Press, 1979. Includes the daily offices in traditional and contemporary English, according to the use of the Episcopal Church.

1982 Catholic Almanac. Ed. by Felician Foy. Huntington, Indiana: Our Sunday Visitor, 1981. This annual publication contains a list of Roman Catholic retreat houses throughout the United States.

Christian Prayer: The Liturgy of the Hours—Morning Prayer, Evening Prayer, Night Prayer. English translation prepared by the International Commission on English in the Liturgy. Collegeville, Minnesota: Liturgical Press, 1976.

Directory of Religious Communities of the Anglican Church in the Americas, A. Palm Desert, California: Society of St. Paul, 1979. A listing of Episcopal orders in the United States and Anglican orders in Canada, many of which schedule retreats.

Doherty, Catherine de Hueck. *Poustinia: Christian Spirituality of the East for Western Man.* Notre Dame, Indiana: Ave Maria Press, 1979. Describes the poustinia or desert experience: a solitary retreat.

Episcopal Church Annual. Wilton, Connecticut: Morehouse-Barlow, 1981. Includes a list of Episcopal retreat centers in the United States.

Garfinkel, Perry. *Retreats: Away-To-Pray Weekends.* Chicago: Claretian Publications, 1977. This booklet explains the difference between Jesuit, Franciscan, Benedictine, Passionist, and Cenacle style retreats, and provides guidelines for a do-it-yourself home retreat.

Maloney, George A. *Alone with the Alone: An Eight-Day Retreat.* Notre Dame, Indiana: Ave Maria Press, 1982. Communion with God is the theme of this eight-part directed retreat, based on Scripture and the mystical tradition of the Eastern Church, with suggested material for in-depth reflection.

Swift, Sister Helen Cecilia. *A Living-Room Retreat: Meditations for Home Use.* Cincinnati, Ohio: St. Anthony Messenger, 1981. This structured series of fifty-five one-page meditations is presented in the format of an eleven week at home retreat together with guidelines for optional group sharing.

Props and Customs

Alphonsus Liguori, St. *Visits to the Most Blessed Sacrament and the Blessed Virgin Mary.* Liguori, Missouri: Liguori Publications, n.d. Thirty-one meditations, written in 1746 and reprinted in modern translation, using scriptural imagery, such as Christ as the living bread, loving shepherd, or the fountain of the world.

Broderick, Robert C. *The Catholic Layman's Book of Etiquette.* St. Paul, Minnesota: Catechetical Guild Educational Society (distributed by Simon and Schuster), 1957. A pre-Vatican II explanation of Catholic religious practices.

Carberry, Cardinal John J. *Reflections and Prayers for Visits with Our Eucharistic Lord.* Boston: St. Paul Editions, 1977. These meditations are "intended to help one pray rather than to be prayers in themselves."

Cassidy, Norma Cronin. *Favorite Novenas and Prayers.* New York: Paulist Press, 1972. The novenas include those to the Sacred Heart, Holy Spirit, Immaculate Conception, St. Jude, St. Joseph, St. Anthony, St. Ann, Our Lady of Lourdes, the Little Flower, and the Rosary Novena.

Dorzweiler, Edwin. *A Scriptural Way of the Cross.* Chicago: Claretian Publications, 1977. A booklet of scriptural quotations and brief meditations on each of the stations of the cross.

Enzler, Clarence. *Everyman's Way of the Cross.* Notre Dame, Indiana: Ave Maria Press, 1979. Stations of the cross meditations in the form of a dialogue between Christ and man.

Evans, Francis (ed.). *New Saint Joseph People's Prayer Book.* New York: Catholic Book Pub. Co., 1980. An encyclopedia of 1,400 prayers, drawn primarily from Catholic private and liturgical devotions, including the Mass, morning and evening prayer services, prayers for special occasions and conditions, saints' prayers, novenas, and blessings, as vell as a selection of prayers from Protestant and Orthodox Christians, Judaism, religions of the East, and of the Americas.

Gilles, Anthony E. *They Were There: Reflections on the Way of the Cross.* Cincinnati, Ohio: St. Anthony Messenger (issue of April 1981). A time machine approach to the crucifixion: first person accounts by Pilate, Simon of Cyrene, the soldier who stripped Jesus of his garments, the man who nailed Jesus to the cross, the good thief, the mother of Jesus, Joseph of Arimathea, and Mary Magdalene.

Gavitt, Loren (ed.). *Saint Augustine's Prayer Book: A Book of Devotion for Members of the Episcopal Church.* West Park, New York: Holy Cross Publications, 1977. This collection of devotions for private use consists of familiar prayers, pre- and post-Communion devotions, stations of the cross, the rosary, Benediction, preparation for confession, prayers for the sick and dying, litanies, and holy hour meditations.

Hardon, John. *A Modern Catholic Dictionary.* Garden City, N.Y.: Doubleday, 1980. A dictionary of Catholic history and practice, including descriptions of special devotions.

Minchin, Basil. *Praying with Icons.* U.K.: Julian Shrine Publication, 1979. The history, symbolism, and a way of praying with icons are discussed.

Wedge, Florence. *How To Spend One Hour With God.* Pulaski, Wisconsin: Franciscan Publishers, 1980. The author suggests dividing the holy hour into twelve segments of about five minutes each—praise, repentance, aspirations, surrender to God, Scripture, reflection, silence, petition, intercession, resolution, contemplation of God within, and thanksgiving.

Materials for Meditation

Bonaventure, St. *The Soul's Journey into God; The Tree of Life; The Life of St. Francis.* Tr. with an introduction by Ewert Cousins. New York: Paulist Press, 1978.

Boyd, Malcolm. *Are You Running with Me, Jesus?* New York: Holt, Rinehart and Winston, 1965. Social commentary prayers.

Calvin, John. *Devotions and Prayers.* Grand Rapids, Michigan: Baker, 1976. A collection of fifty-two one-page reflections, each with an accompanying prayer.

Capps, Walter Holden, and Wendy M. Wright. *Silent Fire: An Invitation to Western Mysticism.* New York: Harper & Row, 1978. An anthology arranged by period, from the early Fathers to contemporary times.

Eckhart, Meister. *Meister Eckhart.* A modern translation by Raymond B. Blakney. New York: Harper and Brothers, 1941. Contains Talks of Instruction, The Book of Divine Comfort, The Aristocrat, About Disinterest, 28 Sermons, Fragments, Legends, and The Defense, by this early fourteenth century German Dominican mystic.

Fenelon, Francois. *Christian Perfection: Devotional Reflections on the Christian Life.* Minneapolis: Dimension Books/Bethany Fellowship, 1975.

Juliana of Norwich. *Revelations of Divine Love.* Tr. with an introduction by M.L. Del Mastro. Garden City, N.Y.: Image, 1977.

Law, William. *A Serious Call to a Devout and Holy Life: The Spirit of Love.* Ed. by Paul C. Stanwood. New York: Paulist Press, 1978.

Lyons, H.P.C. *Praying Our Prayers.* Chicago: Franciscan Herald Press, 1976. These reflections on the Lord's Prayer, Hail Mary, Hail Holy Queen, and Anima Christi can serve as prayers by themselves, spiritual reading, or a springboard to further meditation.

Quoist, Michel. *Prayers.* Tr. by Agnes M. Forsyth and Anne Marie de Commaille. New York: Avon Books, 1965. A collection of prayers and meditations inspired by everyday experiences.

Reinhold, H.A. (ed.). *The Soul Afire: Revelations of the Mystics.* Garden City, N.Y.: Image, 1973. An anthology of mystical writings, organized by subject.

Thomas à Kempis. *The Imitation of Christ.* Ed, with an Introduction by Harold C. Gardiner. A modern version based on the English translation made by Richard Whitford around 1530. Garden City, N.Y.: Image, 1955.

Wisdom of the Desert Fathers, The. Tr. with an Introduction by Sr. Benedicta Ward. Foreword by Metropolitan Anthony Bloom. Fairacres, Oxford: SLG Press, 1977. A collection of short sayings of the Desert Fathers.

Wojtyla, Karol (Pope John Paul II). *Sign of Contradiction.* New York: Crossroad/Seabury, 1979. Based on a Lenten retreat given for Paul VI and the curia in 1976, this series focuses on man's encounter with and acceptance of Christ. Includes reflections on the stations of the cross and rosary mysteries.